Copyright © 2010 By T.B.R. Walsh

All rights reserved. No part of this book may be reproduced, stored electronically, or transmitted in any form or by any means without written permission from TMC Books LLC.

ISBN: 978-0-9720307-8-6

TMC Books LLC.
Conway, NH
U.S.A.

www.tmcbooks.com

Arlene's Book

Two short memoirs and an unfinished
manuscript by Arlene C. Walsh

Introduction

I still remember the phone call. It was a Thursday; I had just gotten home when I recognized the voice on the phone as my father's. Before I could say more than hello, he said he had very sad news: my mother had been killed in a car crash.

I suppose like most people who lose a parent there is a sense of the world turned inside out. The ensuing days were made up of a blur of phone calls, difficult conversations, and flights first to New York, and then on to Santa Fe, to deal with the literal and practical aspects of the end of a human life.

As my father, brother, sister (by phone, since she had a brand new baby), and I struggled to sort through Arlene's possessions and deal with the aftermath of her sudden death—furniture to go here, dishes there, emotional baggage who knows where—the pile that represented her writing took on greater significance. Even before we had finished cleaning out her small adobe house, friends and family were asking if there was any way that her manuscript could be published posthumously. I found myself answering the question with another—which manuscript?

There were poems, parts of several novels, and autobiographical pieces. Most inquiries were for the last book she had been working on, *The Sky's the Limit*, a chronicle of her own process, as an older woman, trying to build an airplane and follow her dreams. Unfortunately, the manuscript for *The Sky's the Limit* was only 45 pages long, and was incomplete, necessarily so, since the plane was only about half finished. However, as we sorted through her papers, we found that there was a skeleton of a memoir.

Arlene's Book is a compilation of three manuscripts. *Pot Roast on the Ceiling,* is a collection of memories from her childhood which she put together when her first grandchild was born. *The Door to the Rainbow* is a collection of observations made in the course of a year teaching in a one-room schoolhouse in rural New Mexico. In some ways the most revealing manuscript, *The Door to the Rainbow,* was written at a particularly happy time in her life and the sheer joy of working with children shines through from every page. *The Sky's the Limit* chronicles her progress building the biplane she was working on at the time of her death; it is a text that is full of reflection about her life. It is also an attempt to sum up the life lessons she felt were important and the values that she believed in.

 I was familiar with the first two manuscripts, and needed only to re-acquaint myself with them and render them into some sort of digital form compatible with the twenty-first century. *The Sky's the Limit,* on the other hand, came as a surprise to me in two distinct ways. One was that it became clear to me that the sudden and tragic death of her fighter-pilot cousin Howard, still haunted her sixty-two years later. After re-reading both *The Sky's the Limit* and *Pot Roast on the Ceiling,* I have begun to wonder if she had ever really come to terms with that death.

 The other area that surprised me was the way that she describes herself at the point in her life when we, her children, were young. She is eloquent in her descriptions of herself as dominated by the roles she was expected to play as mother and wife. She is clear about her feelings of having needs that were not met, even by her, and of essentially feeling trapped. I sense a patina of unhappiness when she writes about this stage in her life. What surprises me is that her perspective of that time is so different from my own. I do not mean to say she is has misrepresented her feelings, only she could truly know what she felt, but my recollections of my mother from that time are of a somewhat self-absorbed person, who was generally happy, and delightfully unconventional.

 I wanted to draw attention to this because when she writes about this time in her life, I think she is selling herself short. Her unique ways of dealing with things and her unconventional approach may actually have made things more difficult for her on some occasions. However, I know that among my peer group, she was recognized first as a distinct personality, and only second as my mother. In short she was "cool."

In the editorial process of this book I have not changed Arlene's words. She felt strongly about many things, and it did not seem right to soften, clarify, or explain her perspective on her own life. After more than two years of trying to pull this project together, I have found that the more I think about it and read her words, the more I appreciate what a complex and passionate soul she was.

I miss her laugh.

Ted Walsh

It was not easy being Arlene's daughter. She was not your conventional mom. Yes, she would make cocoa and bake cookies (that's when I quickly learned to bake). When everyone around us dressed as preppies, we dressed more like hippies, when everyone was consuming red dye #1 (or is it #2?) my mother was preaching its dangers. When everyone's moms were bragging about their kids, my mom was telling us that we could do whatever we wanted, but we had to put our minds to it. And then she practiced what she preached. When I first told my mother that she was going to be a grandmother, instead of feeling old or complaining about getting old, she saw it as an opportunity to do something she had only dreamed of—she began to learn to fly. She dreamed of flying her grandchildren in her own plane. She wanted her own plane, so she began to learn about building one.

My mother never ever said that she was old, she always said that she was getting younger all the time. I would shake my head and tease her about it—maybe a denial of old age? As time passed, I sometimes thought she wasn't kidding. She was always eager to learn something new. She never went on about the good old days, it was always about the present or future. She had big dreams, but she would fulfill them a tiny piece at a time. There was never a doubt that she would finish her plane, at least not in her mind, though maybe in mine. As time passed, and she showed me pictures of her plane, my doubt began to decrease. I began to feel an excitement about my own life, that I didn't have to do everything by the time I was thirty. If my mom could build an airplane and learn to fly in her seventies, then imagine what I could do in my forties. My mom gave me such hope not by words, but by example. I not only began to be proud of her, but started to look forward to my own future with a whole new outlook. Yes, I did at times feel sibling rivalry with the airplane—after all, it couldn't have children, it didn't need it's mom. I did, but I also saw what an inspiration it was, and how happy it made her. The airplane was my mother's biggest lesson to me: live your dreams.

A friend of my mothers told me the other day," your mother is just in a place where she can get a lot more done." I think that's true. But it doesn't mean I don't miss her. I had a conversation with her not too long before she died. I was missing someone close to me who had died, and she said that if I only knew how many souls walked beside me everyday I'd never feel alone. It gave me great comfort then and now. My mother cared about so many people, so deeply, that I have no doubt that when we need her she will walk beside us. If you don't feel her immediately, just wait a minute, it only means an interesting plane is flying overhead, but when you need her, she'll be there.

Amory Walsh Hartman

I had seen copies of Mom's two memoirs, but I hadn't read them closely until Ted took on the task of publishing them. Writing was more than a hobby for my mom; it was a responsibility to her. She would be very happy to see her works published in this way. This book is a fine tribute to her memory.

Every year on Mother's Day, I traveled from Albuquerque to Santa Fe to buy my mom some annual flowers for her small patio garden on Acequia Madre. When I saw her on our last Mother's Day, 2007, her gardens were looking the best they had in a long time. She had decided to work on her gardens as her exercise the two or three mornings she had off each week. She had had an awareness of her heart condition for some time, and she worked hard to try to control her blood pressure. I do not think she knew how bad it was. Even if, in a subtle way, she had recognized the danger, it might have kept her from flying, which would have greatly saddened her. Perhaps it was better this way. Yet, it would be nice if she were still around. I miss her green thumb.

Artie Walsh

Contents

POT ROAST ON THE CEILING
And other memories of a Connecticut girlhood

page 1

THE DOOR TO THE RAINBOW
Life in a one room schoolhouse in New Mexico
page 99

THE SKY'S THE LIMIT
How women can realize their dreams in later years

page 169

Pot Roast on the Ceiling

And other memories of a Connecticut girlhood

Arlene with her pet deer, Bambi. The photograph was taken about 1938 or–39; the man on the right was Arlene's father, Alexander Csech.

1. Sanctuary

When I was a small child, my family lived on a sanctuary out on the Bristol Road, with representative species of birds and animals native to the state of Connecticut.

Nothing remains there today, in that area known as Scott Swamp, except what's left of the building that stood at the head of the trail, and that we called the Shelter. But during the time the sanctuary was open to the public, miles of rustic trails wound through those woods, and along them areas had been fenced for animals, and trees and bushes labeled. Various spaces had also been set aside for breeding, and in an area remote from visitors, a long, double-sided row of structures was known as the "hospital." Most of the building had been done by young men of FDR's Civilian Conservation Corps, and I don't remember it. But I do remember the walkways, the myriad storage facilities and office areas, and I remember the animals.

By the time of my first memories, the sanctuary was a large complex, manned by a host of men whose jobs had either been severely cut back, or had vanished altogether. They were my companions as I learned to totter around, and I was an object of much happy attention. Due to these friendships and the fact that I was a verbal baby, my early speech was peppered with colorful expletives; and by the time I had reached the age of a year and a half, I could snap my fingers and let loose with a string of joyous profanities that might cause a longshoreman embarrassment. When I greeted our gentle visiting pastor in this manner, my father called a meeting and asked the men to please watch their language while I was within earshot.

Profanities too were the particular pleasure of a pair of obstreperous parrots who lived for a while on our front porch. Peter and Robert had been raised on shipboard and then presented to their sailor owner's mother. Although the sanctuary did not usually accept non-native creatures, these verbose lodgers stayed until a suitable home could be found, and during their brief reign, they created havoc. Visitors disembarking from their cars for a peaceful afternoon on the woodland trails were luridly described. Colorful descriptions of the human posterior seemed a particular pleasure, and complaints were angry and frequent. This was especially so since people did not realize the "fowl" nature of their provokers.

A pet crow rode my shoulder when I was a toddler, and became unusually adept at hanging articles of my clothing that I decided I could do without in the apple tree. Sometimes this would include everything but bonnet and shoes.

A raven with a split tongue was also a resident, and habitually greeted my mother with a cheery "Hello, Sweetheart." When she had neglected him for some time, however, and then brought him visitors, he fixed her with a beady eye and shrieked, "Where ya been, ya old soak?"

Various experiments were conducted out of the state offices at the sanctuary. Some involved animal response to human fear and its scent. I often found cages unlatched, and visited foxes, skunks, and even mating raccoons, with no ill effects. One experiment, involving the use of electric bulbs, fooled birds into laying their eggs in the snow, and proved that they used the sun's position to tell them when to mate. The experiment, along with pictures of the "snow eggs," appeared in *National Geographic*.

I wandered those paths, socialized with the animals, and trotted along behind workers and visitors alike. I spent long hours following my father from one end of the place to the other, and I bumped along with him in his smart, new Chevy truck. The feeling of being at home in the outdoors and with animals has continued throughout my life, as well as the suspicion, developed then, that the animals are not quite as far removed from us in intelligence and feelings as we might like to think.

The deer were special favorites. These appealing creatures sometimes became so tame that an escapee would often come to the house seeking human companionship. My pet fawn, called, of course, Bambi, often played with me outside the acre that was kept fenced for the deer. We were steady companions, until the ongoing and serious nature of World War II called away the men and dried up funds. I still remember the huge, red truck that bore him and his companions down the drive and to a zoological park in the city of Bridgeport. Because of the gasoline rationing caused by the war, visits were not possible.

So I was a tall, skinny sixth-grader before I visited the deer at Bearsly Park in Bridgeport. I stood talking to them at the fence when I saw a caretaker dash from the little hut on the hill. He was followed by an enormous buck. The great creature raced across the compound directly to me. The man followed apprehensively.

"Don't put your hands through the wire, miss," he told me. "This is an old man, and even in captivity deer have a leader, and with our herd here, he is it."

I disregarded him and reached through the wire to pet the giant. He licked my fingers and rubbed his head against me through the mesh.

"Do you know where this buck came from?" I asked.

"Most of our deer came from Shade Swamp Sanctuary when they closed. This one has always been called Bambi."

People still came to walk the outlying trails after the sanctuary officially closed, and my father continued to work for the state of Connecticut. And I continued my relationship with the woods and its creatures. I knew when and where the arbutus bloomed, and where the spotted owls lived. I knew the astonishment of lady slippers poking from a pine floor at the end of May, and I knew where blueberries grew. My mother and I spent a day each year picking on Blueberry Hill, and afterward, she canned and made blueberry pies. Their smell meant the last days of summer.

When my father died, my mother and I remained for nearly a year before we found a place in town. The house was eventually moved to Bristol, and all the other buildings are gone. But there are times in my dreams when I return to walk the arbutus-strewn paths of a childhood where sanctuary meant more than a place on the Bristol Road.

2. Birdsong

"FIRST MEMORY"

Wet grasses higher

than a three-year-old's blue overalls. Ahead, on the sanctuary bird path, rubber father-boots pause.

"Listen! Bobwhites. A wild one calling one of ours!"

This way, this way.

Across a field, up stone steps,

through the gate in the bittersweet hedge. Small fists curl on wild strawberries, flesh sweet as the words birds speak. One berry in each hand.

It's the first thing I remember. I have a vivid mental picture of the bridge in Unionville painted orange with primer, which went down the river in the hurricane when I was two-and-a-half, and the birds calling in the morning is before that.

I'm not particularly knowledgeable about birds, but I can't imagine an aubade without them. When, as children, we played that game about what animal would you be, I always chose a bird, because they get together and raise families, but they can fly.

Sometimes during my third or fourth fall, my father took me duck hunting. His friend, Charlie Disbrow, and another friend or two, all went down to the marsh below the Disbrow's place very early one morning. People had been living in the Disbrow's big old house in southern Connecticut and shooting ducks in that marsh since well before the American Revolution, and I had a sense of doing something that people had done before me as I trooped along beside the excited dogs, proud to be taken along with the men.

I must have been seven or eight the summer we had the bird club. Not only was our multi-storied garage possessed of a long, steep staircase made of treads only, but the Bishop's big, yellow barn had one exactly the same.

We took turns, Donna and I, and we met twice a week, once on the stairs in my garage, and once on the ones in her barn. We sat on one tread, poked legs through to dangle, and used the tread above as a desk. We copied names and facts about birds into notebooks, and checked each other. When we exhausted our bird manual, the library provided more information, and we just kept going. I don't know if we learned very much, but it was fun.

Up the winding staircase of the library, an upper room contained a collection of birds' eggs that enchanted us. I guess with today's joyful emphasis on hands-on museums for children, it may seem odd, but we loved those eggs in their glass cases, and I went back and walked along them over and over again.

Donna's father, like my dad, worked for Connecticut Fish and Game, and had a laboratory in their house. The room was windowed on three sides, so there was a lot of light, and although there were rules, and some things we were not allowed to touch, most things we were permitted to use. We examined a lot of things under the microscope the summer of the bird club, but I don't remember what they were. We took a hike or two in the woods to look for birds, and then, just before school started up again, Donna's father gave us a slide show. He had lots of pictures of birds, there were refreshments, and tacit adult approval for what had been a totally self-activated endeavor. It was one of those undertakings rife with the somewhat nutty magic that gives a different flavor to things kids do by themselves. We were lucky to have adults around who pushed us into few organized activities, and who were content to add an occasional extra dimension to those things we did in our copious free time.

One winter evening as my family sat at the supper table, my mother suddenly looked up and gasped.

"Look!" she cried.

The kitchen window onto the back porch, that should have showed blackness, was full of a huge, pure white snowy owl. As we stared, speechless, mother suddenly came back to reality.

"Oh," she said, "it's stuffed."

As if on cue, the enormous creature blinked.

We were on our feet then, running for the door, and out on the back porch we found Jim Bishop, the enormous white owl on his arm. Someone had found it trapped in a barn and rescued it. On the way to releasing it into suitable habitat, Jim had stopped by to show it to us.

There were other games in the Bishop's barn. Upstairs, great piles of storm windows leaned in summer, and there were any number of games for these. One was an elaborate hospital game, with various "wards," that I, as the youngest, was required to be sick in, and "take" terrible choke cherry medicine. Nancy, Donna's older sister, could occasionally be persuaded to play with us in these games. One day during the middle of an "apartment house" game using those windows, Nancy quit. She declared herself too old for this kind of stuff, and just walked out. I was stunned, and Donna furious. Casting around madly for some way to vent her anger, she seized a large, inflated truck tire-tube that we used swimming in the pond, and flung it wildly through the open front space of the barn. There was a pause and then a cry, and we rushed to the aperture that once must have been used to pass hay in and out, and looked. There lay Nancy, flat on the ground, having been ringed with the tire. Of the three of us, I don't know who was most surprised!

At certain seasons, too, masses of cork-studded turtle nets hung from the rafters in that barn. We would climb on and propel ourselves with one foot until the net was wound as tightly as it would go. Then we'd hook the leg up, and spin.

They were simple things, but they are the kinds of things that even today children like to do best. How often I've seen the youngsters I teach, their fancy plastic toys left behind, bound out into the hills around school, and dragging old boards and tires and pipes, build "houses" or "buses" or "hospitals." I sit and watch, and above us fly the ravens and red-tailed hawks.

When my own first child was born, again birdsong marked the event in my mind.

"BIRDSONG"

Once, on some Aegean hill the morning birds
sang the first song they ever sang to Socrates.
In purple choruses the Tuscan hill birds
trilled a first aubade for Leonardo.
And with a little moss-green music,
some plain Concord bird
warbled in the world for Henry David,
who would wind that world on microfilm
and call it Walden Pond.
This morning as the sun came up
on tulips marching in their rows
around the yellow wooden hospital,
I heard the singing of a thousand birds.
Small seedling of my soul, your first, this birdsong.
I wonder why,
as blue and gold of Texas day began,
I heard a thousand birds sing.
For whom, such a song,
bird-twitter of a man?

3. Winter

Winter. Close in. Snuffing like some large, shapeless animal, sifting into cracks, settling. Awake while we slept, creeping, covering us who stayed warm under it, in it, holding us in a time apart.

First came the clear, cold days, still golden in November, but sharp and bright. The first mittens, a new pair, usually ones "Aunt Tillie" knit for me, these were elaborate: reindeer, snowflakes, and always my initials on the palm. One year, she made one red and one green. They said STOP and GO, and I was the envy of every child in the schoolyard.

Later in the season, we ate frozen balls of snow off those mittens, but at first, they were smooth and new and November. There was one year when, before the snow came, Donna Bishop, her cousin Warren Walker, and I built a toboggan run from wooden planks, and waxed our sled runners, shooting down to the sudden stop at the bottom. We ran it over and over, a whole day, elongating the run, re-waxing our runners, making it bigger and bigger while looking up into the clear sky for any chance of snow.

No one was allowed on the pond until Jim Bishop had tested it. Then we could skate. I was four the year I learned, and I remember the day. I kept falling in the bulky woolen snowpants, refusing to give in, determined to do it, until I could stand and glide a little, getting the idea. It felt wonderful, and I moved up a notch in status, more one of the big kids.

You could lie on your stomach on that ice, see the frozen bubbles, the clear black parts, the cracks. It would moan and creak, and you could scrape it with a skate edge, lie down and lick the dust of ice, and get your tongue stuck. Weekends when the ice was right, we skated until the sun began to sink behind the hills at the pond's edge, then we all walked back to Bishop's, which was near the pond, for something hot to drink before we trekked up their hill, across the tracks, past the LaLane's cabins and into our own woods. Behind us, the sky would be going down red, and if I was lucky, maybe my mother was making pancakes for supper.

And then it snowed. Some years, there were blizzards and then the snow was deep. In the early years that we lived on the Sanctuary, the whole long drive had to be shoveled by hand, although later on we used a jeep and plow. I remember walking down the drive between walls of snow vastly higher than I was, unable to see anything anywhere but snow. When these storms were predicted, we shopped: lots of canned goods, dried foods like flour and pasta and beans, and always a new jigsaw puzzle or two to set up on the card table before the fire. Coal would be called for. When the lines went down, as they often did in a big storm, they stayed down, sometimes for weeks, and I went to bed with a candle, and was always sorry to see the electricity come back on.

One year, when the snow was deep, we built a snow-house against one of the huge maples in the Bishop's yard. That pair of trees must have measured at least four feet in diameter each, and we rolled great balls and built outwards. When it was tall enough to stand in, we put old shutters we found in the barn across the top, and a blanket for the door. We left water out in shallow pans all night, and used the resulting ice for windows. We built benches of snow along the sides, and because the snow lasted for weeks, we even ate lunch there once or twice.

There was a winter afternoon when, according to prearrangement, I rode the bus to Bishop's instead of getting off at my own stop. I walked down the long hill to their house, and stomped off snow on the porch and went on into the kitchen. There the snow outside reflected off the cream-colored background of the wallpaper, and changed everything inside utterly. There was the same wood stove, the same solid kitchen furniture Jim Bishop had built, and the same clay head of a man in the window who grew grass for hair, and yet everything shone with a reflected light, white, clear, yet mellow. And it was different. The same house, the same kitchen, but not the same at all.

Sometimes we went sliding on Mr. Coblowski's hill. We referred to it as Cobloblowski's hill, and when the snow fell to just the right height over the corn stumps, the angle of the hill gave a perfect sled run. There were long afternoons on that slope, flopping onto our Flexible Flyers and sliding down the hill. Afterwards there was popcorn and hot chocolate and Sorry at the Bishop's vast dining room table, while the socks and mittens steamed on the radiator, and the whole house filled with the smell of wet wool.

But the best of all the winter games was Mother Prickly. The reason for the name was as unknown to us then as it is now, but it always took place in the pine stand just to the southwest of our house. Each child picked a tree, and that was her house, and there was a great deal of crawling to and fro on hands and knees; there were animal noises we made, and there was the fairytale scent of pines. The rest is difficult to explain. But this game belongs to my notion of winter as surely as it must have connected us with other creatures of the wood who knew no "inside," as well as with a time before our own species felt a sharp difference between inside and out.

The smell of fresh cookies in our warm kitchen later was pleasant, but always anticlimactic, somehow, to children who had spent the afternoon communing with something as profound as the winter woods.

Monday evenings in the winter, the wash that had frozen on the line would be spread out on the living-room furniture until it dried--everywhere, that is, but on my father's chair by the fire. There every night I climbed onto the back of the chair, feet on the arm and balanced while he read, often from the Blue Fairy Book. Long after I was able to read for myself, long after I no longer fit comfortably in that spot, long after I might have been expected to have outgrown such a ritual, it continued. It was the last thing before bed and the prayers I postponed saying in my head, so I could draw in the thick, white darkness of winter and wrap it around myself, sinking slowly into sleep, as into snow.

4. Mrs. Jenner's Kindergarten

In our town, Mrs. Jenner was an institution! She had taught the parents of some of my classmates, and she continued the kindergarten long after my time.

The little school operated out of a cozy brown-shingled cottage with a rose arbor over the gate and a tire swing in the large, grassy yard.

The school had begun as a free school for the children of those who worked for the local girls' finishing school, and it finally opened to town residents.

There were two classes: B for the four-year-olds, and A for the fives. The wide front hall included a row of cubbies where we hung our sweaters or coats, and from which I ran when my mother left me on the first day of school. I bolted down the steps after her. I had never been left anywhere before, but she waved gaily, climbed into our blue Plymouth coupe and drove away. Paul Chauvy held the door open so Mrs. Jenner could retrieve me, and although by the time my mother returned I didn't want to leave, and despite the fact that our families eventually became good friends, I continued to dislike Paul into adolescence.

The school space wasn't large, but it was airy and light, and had blocks, puzzles, mini-furniture painted a shiny dark green, and most importantly for an only child, other children.

It was a comfortable way to begin school. Easy and open: if there were expectations other than that we behave like children, I was unaware of them. If there were restraints on being who we were, I don't remember them. There were turns on the swings, the feeling of sun on your back when you played in the sandbox, graham crackers and milk. I think there was a short ceremonial with both classes each day, where we may have sung something or other, and where different children took turns carrying a large book to Mrs. Jenner from which she read a short bit. It may have been a Bible, but I'm not sure.

At Christmas time, we had a sort of songfest that included our parents, and at which each child was presented with a gingerbread boy or girl, according to sex, with his or her name on it in frosting, and a large naval orange.

Many of the children I met in Mrs. Jenner's kindergarten continued all through school with me. Some still live in the greater Farmington area, and one became godmother to my eldest son, and a lifelong friend.

Gail was called Columbine Two, her mother having been called Columbine as a kindergartner, and I was called Bluebird. Our nicknames felt good to us, and as a teacher of young children myself, I've found that nicknames that evolve from some positive aspect of a child's personality are still appreciated.

At the end of our two years, we were given a ceremony involving a vase of flowers taller than we were, and a lot of running around. Asked what I wanted for "graduation," I was reported to have replied, "A rich ratch." Our family friend "Aunt Tillie" obliged, finding an old watch in a drawer, and I was delighted. It looked great on my wrist, and if it no longer worked, that didn't matter. I couldn't tell time anyway.

What sticks in my mind most about that last day of kindergarten, while hanging over the front porch railing with my friends, was the first of the feelings of endings/beginnings that mark a life. I remember some sense of a feeling of "I won't be playing here again," mixed with more than a tinge of excitement and slight apprehension at whatever was to come.

In the long series of "commencements" that life brings, I never noticed that feeling to change very much. I suppose that in life's final moments, it will be quite a lot like hanging over the porch of Mrs. Jenner's kindergarten. If I'm wearing a watch that doesn't work, it won't matter then, either. And if there's time and I get any flashes, I guess they will be very like those I had then. "I won't be playing here any more," tinged with a feeling of excitement, slight apprehension and wonder at whatever may come next.

5. Magic

In the east, a purple-black blanket of cloud spread across the sky, and over our house it rained. But to the west, the clouds stopped and the sun slid slowly toward the break. By the minute, the world became brighter. I stood in the dining room window watching the rain. Beyond me in his living room chair, my father put down his paper and cocked his head, also looking toward the window. In a burst, the sun exploded into view, underlighting the clouds, turning the rain and the world to gold.

My father leapt from his chair and ran through the dining room.

"Come on!" he yelled, racing on through the kitchen. "Come on!"

I followed him down the back steps, the two of us running like crazies, through the side yard and past the green-awninged windows, around the corner of the house and past the front porch. Gold rain streamed, trees cast indigo velvet shadows, the world heaved and bent into some other dimension.

My father came to a halt, glanced up, and threw out his arms.

"Look!" he cried.

I bumped into him, grabbed his leg, and looked where he did.

And then, for the first time, the poet's heart leapt. Above, the great arc of colors curved away into infinity. I could not believe what I saw!

That was the first rainbow I remember, and it was magic.

Today psychological health workers warn about magic thinking. And surely there is a kind of magical thought that muddies reason and halts positive action.

But magic happens! Good magic. The sort where the joy of the moment explodes into an inner certainty that what can be thought can also be made to occur. I know this, because it has happened for me.

Woven into the fabric of my childhood are unexplained episodes that carry the flavor of what forever exceeds understanding.

One afternoon late in winter or early in spring, I set my favorite toy and companion, my Teddy bear, on the front porch steps and placed three pennies in his lap.

"Go on over to the gas station," I told him, "and get me some gum."

Now we lived in the country, in a house well back from the old Route 6, and the gas station lay far down the road. I was alone, an only child, half a mile from any human except my mother, working away at the back of the house, and unaware at that moment of me or my bear.

All afternoon I played. I dug in my sandbox talking to myself as children who are alone often do. I swung on my swing in the big maple tree. I forgot Teddy.

It was much later, nearly supper, sun slanting in thin but mellow, when I tripped down the front steps and nearly fell over my bear.

He sat where I had left him, in exactly the same position. But the pennies were gone, and across his lap lay three sticks of Doublemint gum.

I was in Junior High, father early and tragically dead, when, with mixed feelings, I began to think about the upcoming prom. Everyone was welcome to go, and all of us planned to, me in my new turquoise dress. I pictured the nosegay my father would have bought from Haworth the florist, and I knew just how it would have looked. Paper doily beneath the small, pastel blossoms, and ribbons trailing. But my father was not here. I was too young for a date; the dress had been a gift from my godmother, and there was no money for the kind of extras such a bouquet represented. I would do without. There would be, my mother assured me, other proms.

Then it was the day of the dance. At dinner time, my mother and I arrived home and climbed the steps to the back porch.

The florist's box lay on the bench. My name had been written across it in the somewhat squared-off type letters my father had favored.

The flowers were exactly as I had pictured. They created the very effect I had thought of, and they were the occasion of many compliments during the happy dance. And my mother and I were never able to discover from where they had come.

Now, where I live, rainbows are a part of the afternoon summer showers. Some years I have counted as many as twenty-five during a single season. But I chase them–running up the ladder onto the roof wherever the sky looks promising, answering the phone to hear a friend cry "Rainbow alert! Rainbow alert!" And sometimes, when there is nothing to see at home, I set out to where more horizon shows. For me, the heart leap, the sense of good omen, persists. I pursue, count and cherish as many as I can. And the life I longed for, rich in work I love to do, in peace and joy and love, slides up my sky and hangs, its colors clear yet blending, leading me, up and on.

6. Friday Nights

Friday nights we went shopping. Mostly this meant groceries, but since the nearest market village was Plainville, one town away, drug store items, articles needed from the dime store, and bakery goods, were also on the list. Indeed, anything we anticipated would be wanted before the next Friday, we planned to buy.

The first major stop was Fulton's Market. Jiggs was grocer, and presided behind the worn wooden counter. In those last days of the "Mom and Pop" markets, before the supermarkets put them out of business, my mother went directly to the counter and to Jiggs, with her list. She'd read out what she wanted, and Jiggs would reach behind him to the shelf, or under the counter, and place the item before her. When the can or box she needed was too high up on the shelf to reach, he used a long-handled pincer apparatus to lift it down. For sweets, Jiggs would walk along in back of the counter as my mother walked in front and pointed out what she'd have. Then it was my father's turn, and he and Jiggs disappeared into the cooler room and together chose any meat, besides the chicken we raised ourselves, that we would be using during the week. Hamburger meat was decided upon whole, and brought out front, where I watched it go through the grinder. Sometimes items from the deli would be chosen then, as well.

For a large part of my girlhood, my mother counted out ration coupons, blue for groceries and red for meat, along with the money. Clothing was also rationed, and I remember that shoes used an enormous number of coupons, and were always a problem.

As soon as I could manage to collect my allowance, I cut out of Fulton's Market and headed for the Five and Dime. In my early years I received a nickel, later on a dime. Little by the standards of today, but at a time when an ice cream cone cost five cents, there were a lot of options for a nickel.

Woolworth's was a wonderful store. The wooden floorboards creaked when you came in, and I headed right immediately. Here was my favorite counter. There were pungent pencils, and pink rectangles of sweet-smelling erasers. Boxes of chalk, glues, tapes, and the crayons. These were always a brand called Blendwell, and I don't remember anything that smelled as good as they did. With a new box, the large, ten cents for 16, the points all still sharp, you would be the envy of every girl in your class.

The back of the store held small cans of paint, tools, electric cords, screws, strange rubber bits, all set out in sections divided by glass, and none wrapped in plastic. There were toys back here too, out of my price range, most of them, but fun to peruse. A hat rack above the hardware even held a few ladies' hats.

In the middle of the store and in the middle of the aisles stood an island. Here were featured seasonal specials and other wonders. Here stood the cash register, and here stood Agnes. Agnes knew me and she knew my mother and she knew how much allowance I had to spend. It was Agnes who saw me spot the sachet, and who held it up for me to admire, and to !et me sniff. It was pale blue, beribboned and trimmed with lace, and it smelled of magic. She told me how it was used. I was enchanted. This was surely the best gift my mother could ever hope to receive in her life, and Christmas and her birthday were both rapidly approaching. Unfortunately, I was still in the nickel phase of my allowance, and it cost fifteen cents. For the next two weeks, I could hardly wait to get out of Fulton's and race down the street to see if the sachet was still there. It was, and on the third week, it was mine! I knew my mother had to find it as beautiful as I did. I don't know how I managed to keep it hidden until the big day, but I did. Every once in a while I took it out to smell, and I told my mother every day what a wonderful gift I had for her. I remember that I was surprised and a little disappointed Christmas morning to discover that she already knew what a sachet was.

The dime store also sold penny candy and paper dolls. The dolls came in books, and for a dime you could have several curly-headed children who could be punched out of front and back covers. All the clothes for them to do anything in the world that a child could possibly want to do could be cut from inside. When they were dressed and ready to do these things, then you were ready to do them, too.

When the shopping was done and all loaded into the car trunk, came the best time of all. With me between my parents on the seat of the blue Plymouth, we headed for home—me clutching Blendwells or paper dolls. Home meant spreading out my treasures and playing until bedtime, and the clean sheets that felt and smelled the way no other sheets have since. It was the best ending to the best day of the week.

7. Trip to the North Pole

I must have been either three or four the year my father took me to the North Pole at Christmas time.

It was night, it was dark, and it was snowing, and we went in the little blue Plymouth coupe, me standing on the seat beside him, holding on to his shoulder. We had been traveling down familiar roads for some time, when my father told me to close my eyes.

"Why?"

"Now the car is going into the magic that will bring us out at the North Pole."

I closed my eyes and kept them closed. My father hummed a little tune. Presently, he turned a couple of corners and the car drew to a halt. He told me I could open my eyes.

I looked around me. Everything was different. We were parked before a small fruit store, and the snowy street around me was a snowy street of the North Pole.

We climbed out of the car, and I followed my father toward the fruit store. On the sidewalk, boxes of oranges leaned against the building, their warm, spicy Christmas smell rising. I stared at them. These then were oranges of the North Pole. We entered.

My dad bought a bag of grapes from the shopkeeper, who seemed to know him, and we ate from the bag together. They tasted like grapes from the North Pole. While my dad talked to the shopkeeper, a man dressed in brown and wearing a cap came in, and stood listening. He was different looking, odd in his manner, a little foreign. I stepped away, wary.

My father nudged me and drew me aside. He bent a little, and spoke from the side of his mouth. "See that man?" I nodded. "He works for

Santa Claus."

I stared. "How do you know?"

"I know him."

We left the shop and stood in the street.

"Where's Santa's place?"

"Not too far. But the road is all snow. You can't get there in a car." "You need a sleigh?"

"That's right. This is the center of the village."

We walked down the street. I looked from side to side, taking in the shops where Santa must come once a week or so for supplies, just as we went to Plainville on Friday nights. On the sidewalk, big flakes of dry snow landed, sparkling with that small glint of crystal in them that snow sometimes has, and that I knew snow at the North Pole would have.

We walked and I peered into shops, some now closed with the night, others busy in a Christmas bustle. Some cars were parked along the curbs.

"People here have cars?"

"Some do. Some have sleighs. Some have both."

"Oh."

He took my hand and we went on.

Down the street we went into a book shop, and downstairs to a lower level, where books for children were set out. The salesman greeted my father. "Hi Al. How's it going?"

My father returned the greeting.

"This your little girl?"

My dad said that I was. He pointed out some of the books to me, and I turned pages. He asked which one I might be interested in having Santa bring. I expressed interest in several, but remained noncommittal. Eventually we climbed the stairs and went out into the street again.

Now we turned, walking back toward the car. It was still snowing. I held out my blue wool mitten, caught some snow and ate it. I knew I was eating snow at the North Pole.

We got back into the car and drove slowly away. I turned, watching the streets of the North Pole recede behind me. Soon they were out of sight, and we were alone in the night and the snow, going home.

8. The Years It Rained All Year

The sun must have come out sometimes during the year I spent in the first grade, but I don't remember it. I can still feel the blue rubber raincoat I wore, and still smell the faintly ocean smell of the "oilskins" that other kids wore. What I really wanted was a raincape, but this was not considered practical. I could actually have used any number of wet weather garments.

That first year in "big school," our class occupied a large, airy corner room with its own exit to the playground, and its own double bathroom. The wooden floors were always wet in the aisles, that year, and the cloakroom seemed always full of dripping raingear.

Nor was that all that dripped. Our first grade (one of two) was presided over by Mrs. B, a mean-spirited tyrant, whose syrupy-sweet exterior proved as thin as it was false. Wallace and I were two children who could do no wrong, and the only two. One or the other of us was charged with bringing the monies collected on "banking" and "victory stamp" days down to the office, and nobody else ever got a single turn. So I was lucky and did not fear her, but her cruelty made any feeling of affection or trust impossible.

Warren was not one of the lucky ones. Warren's father had deserted his young, Long Island family not long before, and his mother had come down with one of those serious but unnamed adult illnesses. So his aunt, who happened to be my mother's best fiend, Hazel Bishop, had taken Warren and his younger sister in with her family, and Warren attended first grade in my class. And nearly every morning during the Pledge of Allegiance or prayer that started our day as we stood beside our desks, hands on hearts, Warren wet his pants. Then Mrs. B flew into a rage, shaming and mocking him before the class. If by chance the flood did not occur, she sarcastically called attention to that. Only as an adult was I able to understand some of the terror that little boy must have undergone in those months before his mother recovered, and was able to send for her children.

The feeling of privilege that was mine as an only child, Mrs. B. exacerbated during that wet year, and made second grade with a good teacher who treated me as she did her other students, difficult. And yet that teacher I liked and trusted.

I again wore a blue raincoat as a college freshman. This one had belonged to a World War II nurse, and it was different. At first, this bothered me, but as the year progressed, and we walked up and down the hill to the biology lab, or the barn that was the student center, or back and forth across Prospect Street, always in the rain, I stopped longing for a tan London Fog like the other girls, and the navy coat became not only a trademark, but also a sign of my individuality. And my spirits remained undampened, as I came to love college life.

Driving my daughter to her freshman year at her college in Vermont, I told her about my freshman year. My old college record player and polo coat in the back seat, I told her how it had rained all year that year. So when it rained all of her first year, she blamed it on me, telling me I'd jinxed her. But like her mother before her, the weather failed to drown her ardor for college life.

Those remain "watershed" years for me. And they are linked forever in my mind with damp clothes, independence, life changes, and an appreciation for the realities of the world.

9. World's Fair

It is Sunday afternoon, and I have fallen asleep on my Aunt Mamie's old brass bedstead while the clock beside me ticks away with its loud, antique tick. At four, I am not aware enough of what a World's Fair is to feel very disappointed at the decision to leave me behind with my father, while my mother, aunt and uncle join our friends, the Adams', in exploring the World of Tomorrow, as set up in Flushing Meadow.

I come awake to my father sitting beside me, shaking me.

"Can you wake up?"

I nod, sensing something is up.

"Good! Then let's get going. You and I are off to the fair!"

I stare at him, rubbing sleep out of my eyes. "I thought it was too much for me."

He laughs. "I think we can arrange it so it won't be."

I yawn.

"We will be back long before they will," he tells me, as he helps me into my dress and brushes my hair.

"But what if we meet the others?"

"There will be thousands of people there, especially on a Sunday. We'll never run into them."

My aunt and uncle live in Bridgeport, and it doesn't take long to drive from there to New York, and soon we are crossing one of the city's great bridges. I stare up into the superstructure in wonder.

My father chuckles. "I bet you'd like to swing around up there."

I nod.

"Maybe you'll be an acrobat when you grow up."

I frown. "Why would I want to be an apricot when I grow up?"

We drive on toward the world of trillion and perisphere.

There are some rides, some small marzipan fruits, and my first stick of cotton candy. We take in an exhibit or two, then stand in line to get into the World of Tomorrow.

Mazie Adams is strolling along with my mother and their group.

"Oh, look at that little girl! She looks just like Arlene!"

My mother looks. "She looks just like Arlene because she is Arlene!"

Amid the thousands, we have managed to cross paths. There are general greetings and a lot of merriment, before the parties go their separate ways. The others have already seen the World of Tomorrow, but my father wants us to see it, so we continue on in the line.

Somewhere we have a snapshot of my mother and Mazie, in that very much more dressed up time, seated on the rim of a fountain in suits and hats. While they sit there, my father and I wait for the World of Tomorrow.

I do remember it. Below us, small cars move on superhighways, their cloverleaves clearly visible. It is the world where I live now, with its mass communication, easy air travel, and color TV on which we can watch the wars we fight even as we fight them.

In some ways, it was all remarkably accurate. But what it did not show was the shadow side. The bright feeling that there would be enough of everything for everyone is gone, and our "good life," that was to bring us so much satisfaction, has managed to puncture not only the ozone layer, but our spirits as well. We are not able to be as in control as we thought we could. The feeling of wonder and hope that is ours, as we exit back into daylight, is gone, and we are running scared. What we've found out about the World of Tomorrow that is today, is that it is all too like the world of yesterday. Terrible, and wonderful. Only more so.

Maybe it would help to look down as we did then, to the earth, understanding that it is our base, our grounding, and where we are. Then we could look up and see the stars over us, the place from which we came and to which we go.

10. Who Trains the Gorillas?

Being a kid isn't easy. The way to adulthood, to some sort of mature understanding of the particular world in which you find yourself, is fraught with misunderstanding. Just learning the language, the subtleties and idioms, is a perilous undertaking. The natural bent of children to substitute a word they know that sounds like one they hear but do not know, coupled with their tendency to make things concrete, further confuses things.

For the first years I can remember hearing the stock market report, for example, I repeatedly asked nearby adults what happened to the tables. I knew somehow what exchange meant, and it seemed that some people wanted to swap their "chairs." But what about their tables?

And how about guerrilla warfare? Radio bulletins repeatedly announced that gorillas had come down from the hills and destroyed something or other, and my question was always the same: "Who trains the gorillas?" Naturally, the response was never satisfactory, and it was not until I actually saw the word in print and went to the dictionary, that I discovered that the sneaky kind of warfare that had served the American colonists so well during the Revolution, had nothing whatever to do with the large, gentle animals who, through the destruction of much of their environment, have been brought so close to extinction.

I was older, already a young teenager, when during the O'Learys' annual Christmas party, a particularly embarrassing moment occurred. Everyone was required to in some way perform, and I stood up in my new Christmas-red corduroy skirt and sang Winter Wonderland. At a certain point in the proceedings, the assembly dissolved in merriment, somewhat to my dismay.

"Great!" boomed Bill O'Leary when I'd finished. His piano accompaniment had slid along beside me while I'd sung. Only later when we were alone in the kitchen with only his old mother rocking quietly in her chair, did he let me know the part of the lyric I'd misssung.

"Arlene," he told me, "It's 'Later on we'll conspire, as we dream by the fire'." He defined "conspire" for me.

"Oh."

It seemed entirely natural to me, if a little odd, to assume the line went: "Later on we'll perspire, as we sit by the fire," and that was what I had sung.

Sometimes it's possible that the misunderstandings cause real trouble. I must have been about seven or so, when the issue occurred about Mr. Pond's feet.

Mostly my father's work for the Connecticut Department of Fish and Game did not involve real hazards. But there were exceptions. One was the time during deer hunting season when my dad arrived home sporting a bullet hole directly through the crown portion of his buff-colored hat. Fortunately, he wore the hat seated quite high on his head and so had escaped injury. He found it quite amusing. My mother did not. But soon after, all state workers who had occasion to be in the woods were issued bright orange caps.

Then, there came the incident of outright thievery at a Connecticut trout hatchery. I had visited the place many times, and was always delighted with the tiny new-hatched silver slips that darted about the inside tanks, and with the succession of outside pools where one could follow the path and see the fish becoming bigger and bigger. By the last pool, they were recognizable as the rainbows used to stock the state rivers and streams.

Trouble had occurred with the actual stealing of the mature fish. This was happening at night, and on an alarming scale. The hatchery had asked for help, and various game wardens and state workers were pressed into service.

The Ponds were friends of ours. They had a large farm in what was then easily-arrived-at Connecticut countryside. Our families visited back and forth, and I remember playing with a series of boys from the state school whom the Ponds took on for the summer to help with farm work. Mr. Ponds had been designated, along with my father and others, to set up an ambush at the trout hatchery on a certain night. There was some excitement and a little apprehension as the evening approached. It was nearly time to leave when Mr. Pond called.

My father put down the phone. "Rick Pond won't be coming," he told my mother. "Says he's sick."

"What's the matter?"

"Didn't really say. If you ask me, sounds a lot like cold feet."

"Really?"

"Yeah," my father told her. "I wondered when I told him about it. I think he might be yellow."

The ambush was a success, the transgressors apprehended and turned over to the full force of the law.

It was not too long after this whole situation had been put right that Mr. Pond dropped by our house.

"How's your feet?" I greeted him, proud that I had recalled to mention his affliction.

"Well my feet are just fine, little lady. Why do you ask?"

"Because I remember," I told him, "that they were bad. I remember the night everybody went out to catch the robbers at the fish hatchery, and you were sick. Daddy said your feet were very cold, and that you were all yellow."

There was some nervous laughter, and an attempt to gloss over the implications of what I'd said, but the visits between our house and the Ponds ceased, and Mr. Pond never "dropped by" our house again.

11. All the Candles in the Church

In the little town where we lived, there were three churches. The Episcopal Church lay just north of the school, small and stone and almost more of a chapel than a church. The Reverend Mr. Harding presided here, and was Rector the way FDR was president—always. To the southwest of the school and in front of the library stood the neat, rectangular Congregational church. Simple and open inside, it was this steeple that could be seen from nearly anywhere in town, and when we were in eighth grade, someone took us up in it, and we discovered that the reverse was also true. You could see all the way to Depot Road to the west, way toward Avon to the north, Dutchland Farms and the Plainville Road to the south, and over to the east way up toward Oakwood. Here, Mr. King was minister.

But most of the time, these were kept locked, and only the Catholic church, a block or so south of the center of town and next to the Porter School's cow pasture, proved accessible. Here, Father Dignam ruled.

I don't know why Kristen Sanborn should have been with me that day, as she was not then a Catholic, but I'm sure it was she who told me about the candles.

For some reason, I seemed not to have really noticed them until then, but there they were. Suddenly bold in my consciousness, racks of them in graduated heights, rising front, sides and back of the church, blinking and leaping in their short, maroon containers. They looked wonderful.

"What are they for?" I asked Kristen.

"They're wishes to God," she said.

"Wishes?"

"Yeah. You decide what you want, light a candle for it, then God looks down and sees your wish burning."

"You can wish anything?"

"Sure, why not?"

It took several days for the idea to germinate, but later in the week, after school and before the second bus, I headed down toward the little church. I'm not quite sure, but 1 think I only meant originally to light a few wishes for special friends, and just got carried away. It amazes me now to think how certain I was of what everyone might need or want, but certain I was. Almost before I knew what was happening, I had the whole bank of candles to the right of the altar ablaze. Still I could think of other things people might want, so I moved around to the side and whipped through those.

At the back of the church, several stands of candles waited, and today I'm astonished that in my six or seven years, I had become acquainted with so many people. Because I remember that I had little difficulty thinking of wishes for what must have been well over a hundred candles, and I lit them all. I lit every candle in the church.

It was one of those times when the several-mile bus ride from school to home lasted forever. I ran up the drive and burst through the back door. I could hardly wait to tell my mother what I knew.

"You know the candles in the church? They're for wishes! You light a wish and God looks down and sees it and maybe it can come true!"

"Did you light one?"

I could hardly hold in the delicious news. "I lit them all! Now everybody can maybe get everything they want. Maybe even the war can be over!" It seems I'd added that one for good measure.

"That's wonderful," my mother said. "What a nice thing to do! How did you pay for it?"

A heartbeat of a pause while the world spun, whirling and blinking in a swirl of wax and flame.

"Pay?"

"Well, you're supposed to put a dime, I think it is, in the slot, for each candle."

I decided to brazen it out.

"You don't need to pay. Kristen said." Actually, it wasn't an outright lie. She hadn't said you did and she hadn't said you didn't. She had neglected to mention it at all.

"Of course you do. Candles aren't like flowers. The glass holders don't grow new candles. Someone has to take out the bits that are left when they burn out, and put in new ones. They aren't free. Somebody from the church has to buy them."

"Buy them."

"Sure. They come in big boxes, I think. When they burn out, the person who takes care of the church goes around and puts new ones in. You didn't pay?"

I was speechless. I shook my head.

"Oh."

I waited, frozen.

"I think you'll need to find a way to pay for them. Otherwise, it's not fair."

I stood. Multiplication had not yet been incorporated into my education, but I could see that if every candle cost a dime, it was clear that I ventured into a world of higher deficit as entangling as ever coal miner owed the company store. I didn't think it probable I would live long enough to pay it off.

I gulped. "My allowance," I said. "For a long, long time."

"Yes. And maybe you can do some extra work around here and earn a little more."

I nodded.

"It was a nice thing you wanted to do."

Another dumb nod.

"But those wishes aren't free. Somebody has to pay to put new ones in place of the ones you burned. Other people might want God to look at their wishes, too."

"I see."

"I'll help you keep track, so you can pay."

"Ok."

We kept track, more or less, and I eventually managed restitution on the greater portion of candles used.

So it is, when one tries to tell the gods what to do. Not only may their time schedules not coincide with yours, but also it may be only after the fact that you discover the price.

12. Halloween

What could be better than the whole world setting up a ritual night just for us kids? Halloween was like that when I was a child, and like every kid I knew then, and like every kid I know now, I loved it.

Although I remember my mother driving me into town the year I was four, and I saw her slide behind a tree as I mounted the steps to my teacher's house, it wasn't very long before I was allowed to join a roaming group of my peers, who could canvas almost the entire length of Main Street on Halloween night. Sometimes we might sport "boughten" masks, but even in those cases, the majority of our costumes were usually home-concocted, and often vastly original. Gangling trees, packages of cigarettes, animals of every sort and stripe, as well as all manner of ghosts and bandits, roared along the streets, largely without ill intent, and entirely without fear.

Sometimes host families invited each visiting group in, asked each child's name and where she/he lived, and invited every youngster to explain his or her costume. This was rather fun, but so was racing along the street, running from one side to the other, examining the take from each house. One year, in a particularly wicked mood, we decided to do something "bad," but in the end had to forego the idea, because we couldn't think of anything. Another year (I must have been in about fifth or sixth grade), I joined my friends Margi and Siddy up in the East District. We connected with a larger group and set out on a real marathon. When one of the slightly younger boys soaped the screen of a woman who had already treated us, we took him aside and did what we girls usually did to keep order among those creatures of what we considered a decidedly inferior sex—we beat him up.

On a particularly mellow Halloween, when I was in Junior High, I dressed in an elaborate antique costume, and braved the long distances between houses in my own rural district. With a group from this part of our sprea-out town, I must have traveled some ten or twelve miles before we quit, exhausted.

My own children were just as enchanted by Halloween, and one son even needed to be admonished not to speak during his last year of trick-or-treating, as his voice had begun to change.

At the end of each Halloween evening came the glorious tally. Then the night's loot would be poured out onto somebody's living room rug, lined up, counted, and traded. Then of course, a piece or two from the sticky jumble would appear in each lunch, almost until Christmas.

I can revive that spooky flash of familiar excitement even today as I hear my young students planning costumes, or help them count off days on the calendar until the bewitching night. Tales of poison or razor blades may sharpen parental concern, but seem to do little to dampen the enthusiasm of children. Given moderate freedom in accordance with their ages, and some discrete supervision, children do create their own magic as they go.

13. Ironing American History

Ironing is supposedly the least favored household activity among American women. I once knew someone who reached the bottom of her ironing basket, and discovered a magazine from 1967.

But I have never particularly minded ironing. When I was little, Monday night was ironing evening, and my mother set up the board my father had made for her when they began housekeeping, and went to work. My school dresses (jeans and overalls were then for weekends only) came off the board crisp, ties hanging. Sheets were ironed as well, folded into fourths to fit on the board. On Fridays, the old top sheet got turned upside down, and tucked in, and became the bottom sheet. Then the fresh one went on top. If there is a more luxurious feeling than slipping into such a fragrant envelope, I have yet to discover it!

But on Monday nights in those days before permanent press, all the dampened rolls sat on the kitchen table under cover, while one by one, my mother reached for them, shook each out, and turned it into a dress, shirt, or hankie. Behind her, the radio hummed, and because it was Monday, Cavalcade of America played, sponsored by DuPont, "Better Things for Better Living through Chemistry." Madam Curie discovered X-rays, George Washington paced beside his freezing men at Valley Forge, the Star Spangled Banner got written, and Alexander Graham Bell invented the telephone and called his assistant in from the next room, all while my mother ironed. To this day, the scent of something fresh from the ironing board engenders in me a mad desire to recite, "Four score and seven years ago . . ." or to burst into a chorus of "Tenting Tonight."

In the spring, I was given another exposure to American history. My father would keep a keen eye out for the moment when the fields along Meadow Road were plowed, and then he and I could go hunting Indian arrowheads. These might have been brought to the surface as the soil was turned, and we'd walk along the furrows with the pink air full of the sounds of birds and the smell of new earth, while he told tales from history. Sometimes these were local: how the Tunxis Indians, whose triangular flint pieces we sought and often found, had lived, and where they were buried. He told about the outlaw Will Warren, his den on Farmington Mountain, and how he eventually came to be hanged in the town square. He recounted for me the arrival of Theodore Roosevelt at the old Farmington Station, and how he traveled past by buggy, to visit a sister who lived on the corner of Meadow Road and Main Street. Listening, I discovered how the former president had tramped our woods and studied our birds.

  At times he told ghost stories. My favorite was always the one about when old Bill Lawrence was working with a road crew that had to move a cemetery. They had dug up the lead casket of a British soldier who had been killed during the Revolution, and were sitting around it eating lunch, and speculating what he might have been like. One dare led to another, and they at last agreed to open it. Rather more effort than they expected was needed, but finally there was a great kind of sucking pop, and the lid came away. And there he was. A bit blue in the face after being dead so long, but perfectly preserved, in his red coat and black boots. They stood in wonder, marveling at his condition. They guessed that some kind of vacuum might have somehow formed, since the pop they heard reminded them of a can of coffee being opened. Even as they spoke and right as they watched, he faded and vanished before their eyes. A few minutes exposure to the air, and all that remained were his outline in ash, the buttons on his jacket and the buckles of his boots.

  These were tales for a child as the first stars appeared, and we stopped looking down and looked up. If the spring moon should rise, we'd look to see if we could make out a face, and once, as we headed across the field toward the car, I saw something on the moon I insisted looked like a footprint.

Alexander and Anne Csech, Arlene's parents. Her father felt that "Alexander" sounded too much like an "immigrant" name; he went by Al, and told people his name was Albert. Arlene's mother's name was Anne, although her name appears on their marriage license as Anna. Her middle name was Margaret. She was known as "Peg," and later in life as "Shecky."

14. The Library

In our town, the library was a place of comfort, if not one of peace. It stood kitty-cornered across the driveway from the school, and children were always welcome there. It was run by the Misses Scudder, who called to each other joyfully from one end of the building to the other, and who always greeted a child with a look of surprised pleasure. The only thing I remember being discouraged from doing was running inside.

The children's wing had floor-to-ceiling windows and a semi-circular bay with sofa at one end. The number of books seemed extensive for the town and the era, yet I must have gone through a goodly number of them before I moved to the adult rooms. My friend Gail devoured the whole lot.

On snowy winter afternoons, a fire burned in the huge fireplace, and minus our boots, we were allowed to curl up on one of the two great sofas flanking it, and read.

There were story hours, not only one for the small children who always seemed to get read to anyhow, but one for us older kids, where "chapter" books were read out in installments. It was fun even if we could rarely keep from racing ahead to find what happened, on our own.

The Scudders never seemed to find us or our questions annoying, and were forever full of enthusiastic ideas as how we might find answers to them. They showed us how a library operated with the air of letting us in on a great secret, and so it felt. I think that may have been the only time anybody in the building whispered. I remember my faint surprise upon discovering that the library belonged to all the people in the town because it felt the way our school felt. It was ours.

In the seventh grade, Margi, Siddy, Norma and I organized a

Writers' Club, and we were given our own special table and chairs, tucked away under the spiral staircase in the front hall. Since the front hall received scant use, it reeked of privacy and privilege, and told us in ways that words could never have, that writing was an OK thing to try to do. One of the Miss Scudders presented us with bunches of number two pencils, which she informed us, were the very best for writers to use. We met there to write, exchange ideas, read our works to each other, and giggle, and we did it on and off for more than two years. It was there I composed my Last Will and Testament, although to my mind, that document was too important to be entrusted to a number two pencil, and was carefully inscribed in purple ink. As I remember, most of the items mentioned were to go to other members of the Writers' Club in the event of my untimely demise, including some pairs of fancy underwear. If we usually outgrew the ambitious tomes we wrote before they were completed, still we acquired practice, some skill, and a real idea of the joys and agonies of attempting to express one's self through words. Today, the buzz word for the way we felt is "empowered," and that's what the Writers' Club did for us. We learned that writing was worth doing, and that we could do it.

By the time I was in high school and had begun to win a prize or two for writing, the Misses Scudder had retired, so I was unable to share this with them. But I hope that wherever they went, they took with them a sense of pride in their accomplishments. And one of those accomplishments surely was to have given a whole generation of the town's children the idea that "library" meant not only a place where books could be borrowed, but also one where ideas, information, stories, skills, and fun were ours to keep.

15. Summer

Like that glorious, primordial Saturday morning of Tom Sawyer, summer was come. It came in a blast, rich with sun and fragrant with flora. It came in a rush, rife with eraser crumbs as we cleaned up our textbooks for "those babies behind us," and it came wild with plans so multitudinous as to be exclusive of each other. And it came too on tiptoe that first morning you wandered into the kitchen still in your pajamas and stood staring out the back door, opened up now like time itself, and watched the breeze of possibility stir in the apple tree. You could feel forever itself waiting under your bare feet.

In those days of relatively unstructured lives for children, there was always TIME. I had TIME to climb into the fantasy world of my sandbox, TIME to scramble up into the maple tree above it and sit there, TIME to swing endlessly on the swing suspended from its branch. There was TIME too, to follow around the college boys who painted our outbuildings one summer, taking a turn with the paint, having small balls of putty dropped down my back. There was TIME to march up and down the drive with an umbrella opened to each segment a different color, or to splash in a metal tub wearing a blue wool swimsuit with three waves embroidered in yellow on the bodice.

There were the little joys of summer: lemonade poured from a pitcher into glasses that all bore concentric circles of rainbow colors in descending order; ice cream in cardboard cups, that was eaten with a small wooden spoon and from which the milky film could be licked. Then the paper was peeled away to reveal the picture of a movie star, Roy Rogers and Dale Evans, Fred Astaire, or, if our luck really held, Margaret O'Brien. Hot afternoons, I could plan with friends out in the shelter, or on the cool linoleum of my bedroom floor. A little older, I could curl into the old couch on the front porch, and read.

And there were the bigger joys. For several years, I attended day camp at the local Community Center, near our school. We walked to various local swimming pools whose owners donated their use, and we swam ourselves silly. Back at the Center, we bashed thick items out of clay, and braided gimp. We sewed books, and took a field trip to Hartford to actually see books bound. We loved it!

There was Bluebell. She was my fat-tired, light blue girl's bike, and on her I rode out into the world, and into my dreams. Down the Depot Road to the top of Meadow Road, from where it was possible to coast for at least a mile at perfect cruising speed before it was necessary to turn and walk back up. Hazel the horsewoman also lived down near the end of Depot Road, and it was possible to visit those magical creatures and dream of the day when five dollars would be saved, and you could ride. In the other direction, I could cross Bristol Road and head toward Plainville. There, off a side track, I could lie beside my bike in the grassy field and watch for planes to take off or land. Sometimes they did. I could head for the Bishops and endless hours of play in the piney woods or the barn. Sometimes I roared back up the Depot Road like some mad person, thunder behind me, shrieking with the joy of racing the rain.

Once, I was followed nearly the whole length of the Depot Road by a man in a car who questioned me as to where I was headed and when due to arrive, but aware of my mother's tales of children's dismembered bodies found on lonely roads, I answered in monosyllables and pedaled furiously.

And there was swimming. Mornings I was on my own, as my mother insisted she needed this time for household chores, but every afternoon that it wasn't raining or she wasn't canning, we walked over to

Bishops, collected their girls if they were not already in the water, and headed out back to the pond. Dug originally for fish storage, its limpid brown waters seemed always the right temperature. We stayed in all afternoon. My father, ever cautious about his only child, had been traumatized as a boy by the drowning death of a teenaged brother, and insisted my mother accompany me. She often brought needlework or a book, and seemed to enjoy it.

Crossing the small footbridge that led to the pond's path, we often picked small water or garter snakes from the trees where they sunned themselves, and wore them like necklaces or bracelets. Some actually became quite tame. But mostly we just swam. Diving from the small cement dam, swinging out and dropping from a rope tied to a shoreline tree, splashing on rubber inner tubes, hour after hour, afternoon after afternoon, we swam the summer away. Inspired by stories in my girls' magazine, I practiced diving endlessly.

"Warren," I remember asking Donna's cousin, "When I dive, do I look like a dime slipping into a slot?"

Warren seriously contemplated a couple of dives, then gave a slight shrug and a shake of the head.

"Looks like Arlene diving to me."

Homeward bound, we stopped at the Bishops. While my mother and Hazel caught up on the gossip, Donna and I sat on the warm stone of the well cover and talked about life.

When Donna, three years older, had friends her own age around, I struggled to keep up. Once a pal informed her after a swim that her eyelashes looked "sterling" when they were wet, and I seethed, later using the dictionary to no avail. Donna thanked her seriously.

In hot weather, suppers were simple and "something cool." Then, once it was dark, my family and I, and anyone who happened by, headed to the front porch. There we sat by the hour, looking out between the great trees at the yard edge to the road. There the cars went by slowly, and sometimes my father sang. Dreams were dreamed while fireflies flashed over the grass, as silent as the stars up there, their light as soft as the softness of the night itself.

Arlene and her mother.

16. Pot Roast on the Ceiling

Every era has its culinary fashions. Not only food, but also the latest, most modern implements in food preparation come and go. And although there are a few still in use today, pressure cookers were the "must have" of my girlhood. These heavy iron monsters rode proudly atop all the stoves of my memory, spitting and hissing with what looked to me an obvious ominous intent. But they were not just tolerated; they were revered. They were the Cuisinarts of their day.

As popular for cooking the evening meal as they were for the annual jarring up rituals that terminated the victory garden season, and were referred to as "canning," they also sterilized baby bottles, and slow-cooked or fast-cooked (I was never quite sure which) the Sunday dinner. Sometimes this was known to occur when the more confident of their users were at church.

The Bishops were at home one Sunday while their pot roast fizzed away on the stove. Hazel Bishop was occupied in her pantry, that glorious, spice-and-stored-food smelling room adjacent to the kitchen that has long been replaced by matched sets of cupboards whose shelves are so high I can rarely reach more than the bottom one, and whose looks remind me of nothing so much as rows of baby coffins.

She was summoned back to the kitchen by the unmistakable sound of an explosion, followed by a huge "thwonk." The kitchen she found full of steam rapidly condensing into water droplets that covered everything. As she made her way to the stove, she spotted the cooker through the fog, now quite topless, but still bubbling away. She followed the sound of dripping upwards and there was the pot roast, its topmost part effectively converted into a giant suction cup, fastening it securely to the ceiling.

"Jim!" she called. "James! Come here!"

Donna and Nancy's father came through from the other room. She pointed and he looked. The steam was clearing now, and they could see gravy dripping down the wallpaper above the stove. Jim managed to disengage the errant machine from its heat source, and when the initial fright began to dissipate, they started to laugh.

So was born one of their family legends, a story repeated down the years by friends as well. In those days, before vinyl wallpaper, the gravy stains were there to stay, and they did. Nobody seemed to mind. It was years before that paper was changed, and anyone caught glancing at it provided yet another opportunity to tell the story of the day the pot roast ended on the ceiling.

17. Going to Pennsylvania

Today we are a nation of travelers. We hop on planes so frequently that the small city airports we once knew have grown to international proportions, and our continuing love affair with the automobile has landed us in serious planetary difficulty. Our children routinely study abroad—one of my sons spent a summer immersed in art history in Florence, Italy, for less money than it would have cost him for a semester at his university, and I spent two and half years commuting from Boston to New York City on a weekly basis.

But we live now on a shrunken planet. In the world of my childhood, before common travel by plane, before the construction of the interstate highway system, taking a trip assumed titanic proportions.

My mother was born in a small mining community in eastern Pennsylvania, and until the time of her death, some eighty-two years later, she communicated regularly with members of the extended family who remained there. When I was growing up, our family made visitations whenever it could, but those two hundred odd miles were not traveled lightly.

For months before, letters passed back and forth finalizing all details. (A long distance phone call then meant nothing less than a death.) For a week, bags had been packed, lawns mowed, and arrangements made with neighbors to feed animals.

On the morning of the trip, we rose early, four or five o'clock, and breakfasted as quickly as possible. We wanted to be on the road by sunrise. Suitcases had been loaded into the car the night before, and a special trip made to a nearby town to fill the car with gas. As night turned to day, we were off.

No heading for the nearest superhighway ramp for us then; they didn't exist. We turned toward Plainville, and drove through its still sleeping center in the first light. It was the beginning of the incredible number of towns and villages we would be obliged to pass through to reach our destination. On we drove toward New York, the sun full in the sky now.

On some trips, we stopped at a restaurant or hot dog stand for lunch. I remember once when I was very small, a wide, green lawn with umbrellas, but the best thing of all was a picnic to be eaten at the Bear Mountain Bridge, high in the Catskills. There was always excitement as the car wound around the mountain roads, and we waited for the first sight of the great bridge. There were several stops to view it through the coin operated telescopes before the final excited crossing. Look up! Look down! Once over, we pulled to the side and parked, then back along the walkway to somewhere near the middle. I always took along a couple of stones to toss over the side and watch on the way down. Below us, boats went up river or down, their wonderful wakes triangling out behind, and the vessels themselves no bigger than toys.

Back on the road, the long afternoon wound around us, as we rolled through farm country, green with pasture and bright with cows.

We sang. Funny songs, happy songs.

"California, here I come," I bellowed. "In a small blue car with a big bass drum! Gonna boom boom and boom boom tonight."

My parents laughed. We stopped for ice cream. Grew sleepy. Sometimes I leaned into one of my parents as I sat between them on the front seat of the Plymouth coupe. Now the grass disappeared, the land took on that arid look of coal country. At about three or four in the afternoon, we slid down the last of the hills that led into Freeland, and drew up before my cousin's.

They would be in the yard as the car drove into sight, yet they never ran toward it, but raced on into the house in a tumble, screen door slamming, shouting as loudly as they could, "They're here! They're here!"

Then we were among the leaping children, escorted on into that house that always smelled of baking bread, and I was once more in the world of jacks on the porch, hide and seek in the cinder-covered back alleys at dusk, and walks "uptown," where every ice cream parlor would be visited, and where all the cars along the curb bore out-of-state license plates.

There were visits to yet more cousins in the neighboring village of Jeddo, where some of them owned a store, and where once, when quite small and confronted by some twenty-odd cousins, all older, and who were making more of a fuss of me than I could handle, I panicked as they were showing me their playhouse built in the latticework under the house, and impulsively locked them all in.

Back in Freeland, each night was a huge pajama party, often held in the empty third floor on mattresses, and replete with lots of food, bottles of pop, and endless ghost stories.

My mother kept in contact, and continued visiting, taking rides with friends, as the years went by.

Then, in what turned out to be the last year of her life, I got the idea to take her back to Pennsylvania one more time.

Again in a small blue Plymouth, we started early. But it was not dawn this time, and we took the interstate. At least we took the interstate until those final mountain roads that led to the Bear Mountain Bridge. It was no longer the shortest way, but it was what we wanted to do. We stopped to look through a telescope, but the bridge seemed smaller somehow, and without some of its former sense of drama. We ate in a restaurant instead of picnicking, but accidentally took a country road that turned out to be a shortcut, where we passed wild and beautiful pastures, from one of which our passage was watched with interest by a lovely doe.

My mother loved that trip and that visit. We saw the remaining relatives, and I hit upon the idea of asking to see their family snapshots to find out about my background and my forbearers. In the process, I discovered that my grandfather had been the local storyteller, and that my great aunt Annie, a pillar of her community, had arrived in this country at fourteen as a stowaway!

Near the end of our visit, my mother and I went "uptown" to get a few things from the drugstore. Passing a shoe store, she saw a pair of shoes she wanted to buy, but when she went in to ask the price, she discovered she hadn't enough money. She looked across the street at the bank. "Well, I'll just go over and cash a check."

"But they won't cash an out-of-town check," I told her.

She whirled on me. "This is my home town!"

"You haven't lived here since you were fifteen! That's a long time ago."

My mother did not find it funny. "Don't be ridiculous!" She stomped out of the shoe store and crossed the street into the bank. She went up to the window, swung her purse onto the counter and leaned in. "I need to cash a check on a Connecticut bank," she told the young girl behind the glass.

The girl was shifting uneasily, when a voice assailed us from the rear of the building.

"Aunt Peg! Is that you?!

"Yes," called my mother to the disembodied voice. "It's me."

A woman came toward us from the back. "You're staying up with our Aunt Vic. How is she doing?"

"Not too bad. You know. But it's hard."

"Yes. It's too bad about the arthritis." She motioned toward the girl behind the teller's window. "Do you know who this is? This is our Veronica's girl, Leslie."

"No!" To the girl, "How's your mother?"

"Good. She's good."

"That's good. Tell her I was asking for her. I need to cash this check from Connecticut."

She was met by a series of pleased assents, the cash was delivered and more gossip exchanged. Twenty minutes later, we were back in the street and headed for the shoe store.

My mother half turned to me and looked down. "Humph!" she grunted. "I told you. This is my home town!"

18. Dish Night at the Movies

I think it was Tuesday night, and I think it was always raining. My mother was willing to drive, but she preferred not to go alone. So one of the neighbors usually went along: sometimes Beatsie LaLane, and once or twice Mrs. Prezech from down the road. It may be hard today to believe, but I think that in those end-of-depression, start-of-World-War-II days, Dish Night was considered quite a good deal. There was the usual double bill, and for the modest price of admission, each moviegoer was presented with a free dish. One week, a dinner plate, another a cereal bowl, etc., until consistent attendance rewarded one with a complete, or nearly complete, set of some rather heavy but colorful crockery service. Dish Night was not only a local promotion, but I believe it happened all across the country. To this day, I suspect there are cupboards in towns everywhere that still contain a piece or two from Dish Night.

Because the majority of the audience on that night tended to be feminine, I think that the main feature tended to be some romantic opus. I have no way to tell for sure, the double bill running, of course, well beyond my bedtime on a school night, but from the sound of it, the second films seemed always to be similar to each other—a suspense-filled thriller, usually involving Nazis whose cruelty and stupidity always took a losing role to American courage, quick wittedness, and smart-aleck remarks.

I know this because, for me, the dividend from Dish Night came the following morning. At breakfast, my mother recounted for me this second feature in elaborate detail, complete with suspenseful pauses and appropriate vocal dramatics. When she paused for a sip of her coffee, I would draw in my breath and whisper excitedly, "And then what happened?" waiting, breath held, eyes on her face, for the continuation.

There always seemed to be motorcycle chases, night parachute drops, and other hideously dangerous situations, one after the other. And my mother was good at spinning it out, at elaborating, at recounting the tale with exciting embellishments. She took her time, and it was a straight, exciting narrative, well told and well received.

My mother loved to tell stories. She told often of her Pennsylvania coal-mining country childhood, or her teenaged "flapper" years. If in her last years, she sometimes told the same story with a different ending for a desired effect, that came to seem like a more or less natural outgrowth of an active imagination and a very great liberty with the truth.

It's been only lately that I've begun to understand that my love of narrative goes back not only to the nightly excursions into fiction heard from the arm of my father's chair, but also to those wet Wednesday mornings, when I dragged up one of the kitchen chairs, that stand today in my daughter's New York apartment, glued my eyes on my mother as she helped herself to a second cup of coffee, and in delicious anticipation asked, "What was the first movie about?"

19. World War II

When I was very young, there was a war.

Now, World War II is spoken of as the last black and white war, and today that seems true in a double sense. Not only were Americans really sure who were the good guys and who the bad, but also the films that came to us from the front via the newsreels came in actual black and white.

Years after it happened, I remembered riding through a sunny Sunday with our friends, the Adams'. We moved easily past the yellow grasses of December, and the symphony that played from New York filled the car and the afternoon. Then the music was interrupted.

"I'm surprised you remember that!" my mother told me when I asked her, years later. "Yes. That was the news of Pearl Harbor."

But I remembered it. It was the adult reaction that stuck in my mind. It was the first time I had seen grownups afraid.

Life as I had known it changed. We lived now on something called the "home front," where meat, butter and shoes were scarce, gasoline scarcer, and war worry a part of every day.

Now we saved our fat drippings in tin cans on the back of the stove, and when we marketed, turned it into Jiggs, the grocer. Eventually, it was used to help manufacture ammunition. Now when we fried eggs, I pretended they were Axis leaders, and stood by the stove to watch Hitler and Tojo writhe and sputter.

"Whistle while you work," we sang in the schoolyard.

"Hitler is a jerk."

"Mussolini, he's a meanie,"

"Tojo is a dope."

My father listened to every newscast he could tune in on our big, arched, wooden radio, and brooded at what he heard. On Friday nights, we shopped and marketed, and brought Life magazine home, where I tossed it down on the living room floor, and turned its pages of suffering. All that was happening oceans away, but we feared the potential of German technology, there on the East Coast, and staged air raid practice, complete with sirens; cars pulled to the side of the road in darkness, and remember my father's silhouette in his air raid warden helmet, out in the street.

Sugar became scarce too, and bubblegum for some reason, vanished. Everything we wore or ate was expensive or rationed, and what we needed to live, we accepted as being on short supply "for the duration."

At first, the war news was bad, and then it got worse. We sat in our kitchen and listened, as President Roosevelt's high, patrician voice—the way a president was supposed to sound—told us not to lose hope. My family didn't, but they were pretty scared.

When we had saved up enough gas to make a trip to Bridgeport to visit relatives, we wound our way through village streets counting stars in windows: blue for men serving in action, silver for those who had been wounded, and gold for the dead.

We children overheard rumors of an "ultimate weapon" the Nazis were thought to be preparing, perhaps, we told each other on the school bus, to blow up the world.

And my three older cousins learned to fly, and then joined the Air Corps. Bud, the oldest, flew transport Raymond, the youngest, flew army personnel, sometimes "top brass" who marveled at his youth; and Howard, the middle one, flew P47s out of England.

It was to Howard that I felt closest. He appeared at our house during any furlough he could get, often with assorted flying buddies in tow, all of them prepared to eat my mother's famous chicken and dumplings. Because my mother "canned" some of the chickens we raised, she could have this meal ready in minutes on nearly any scale required, and in those days before fast food restaurants, this was considered a wonder, and Howard loved to show her off.

He would sit on the linoleum of our kitchen floor while she cooked, helping me cut out paper dolls and telling his latest adventures, using his hands as planes, the way pilots invariably do. He was cheerful and cocky and carefree, full of the dauntless panache peculiar to airmen of that time, and he could talk about fear, what it did to your body, your reason, and how it tasted in your mouth. He was totally fatalistic.

"Either a bullet has your name on it or it doesn't."

I adored him.

He was shot down three times.

Once over the Channel, his Luftwaffe opponent followed him down strafing him as he climbed out. He went under and held his breath, but when he came up, the German was still there, still shooting. Finally, he dived under his still-floating plane, and coming up on the other side, eluded his adversary. Twice he was shot down over enemy lines, once in France and once in Germany. Each time he was smuggled out by the Underground. From Germany, it took three days, sleeping in barns by day, and walking all night. He always flew again.

Once he had his plane secretly stripped of its armor in order to gain speed. A Nazi pilot, his plane so adorned with flags representing destroyed Allied aircraft that he had been nicknamed "Washboard Charlie," had been a goal for a long time, and the removal of the extra weight gave Howard the extra maneuverability he needed to dispose of "Washboard Charlie" once and for all.

Then, slowly, the news was better. Howard's wing led a D-Day squadron, and the Allies inched across Europe. There were pictures of Paris, its streets lined with crazily cheering citizens, as "our boys" rode their tanks between them. On into Germany the Allies crept, across the Rhein, and into Berlin itself, blood all along the way.

Then it was over in Europe, V-E Day. We held our breath, remembered the dead piled on the beaches of Iwo Jima, and thought about invading Japan, and what was to come.

Howard came home. He appeared at our house on a Wednesday, jauntier than ever, still in uniform, and full of plans to go fishing with my father the following Wednesday. On Saturday, he took up a small plane witha young friend, and they flew into the side of a mountain. I learned then about death up close, and how it can wait for you where you least

Howard

expect it. And about life, and its bittersweet taste on the tongue.

And then came the bomb! We knew it was a good thing, because of the lives it saved. We were a long way from thinking of Japanese lives. When you fight a war with another country, you have to learn to hate that race, and not think of them as people. Or anyhow, not the same kind of people. And we didn't yet know that Robert Oppenheimer had watched the first atomic explosion and quoted, 'I am become Death'.

And then it was over.

Through the wild, mad joy of that night, my parents and I drove, wondering, laughing, weeping, joyous and sad, knowing everything now, and yet knowing nothing.

One autumn evening a few months later, my friend MaryBeth took me into her bedroom to "show me something." I don't remember if it was a **LIFE** anthology or not, but it was that kind of book, a thick, pictorial history of some kind. She held it open at the pictures she wanted me to see.

I looked.

Skin-covered skeletons stood nearly naked, looking out from the pages, but seeing nothing, their faces expressing a blank anguish so deep and terrible that it seemed barely recognizable as human. Other pictures showed bulldozers pushing piles of the skeletal dead toward mass graves. On one page, an immense pile of children's shoes lay heaped; their owners had been gassed in fake showers and then burned in ovens.

"What do you think?" MaryBeth wanted to know.

I shook my head, speechless.

"No, really. What do you think?"

"I don't believe it."

"What do you mean, you don't believe it? I showed you the

pictures. It happened during the war. The Nazis did it."

I shrugged my shoulders. "I know it happened. Still, I just can't believe it."

Later I would learn that I was not the only one to respond this way when confronted with evidence of the depravity to which one human being can sink in inflicting torture on another.

And yet it had happened. The war had happened. And now it was over. Innocently, I had thought things would be as they had been before the war. Now I saw that nothing could ever be the same. The war had taken us down a different road, and that place and time that was "before the war" was somewhere that we couldn't get back to. Like that part of my childhood, I would never be a child in quite the same way again.

20. What Goes Around Comes Around—or—The Poor Girl and the Doll

The developmental school of thought that holds humans to be inherently good must have been begun by people who were never kids. Children are deeply fearful of, and will instinctively attack, that which they see as different. The foreign is always a threat, and is usually met with hostility, often cruelty. Children need adults around to monitor them and take the time and trouble to explain about differences. Then they can begin to lose their fear, and to understand and accept those who are not like themselves. It would be nicer if human children showed instinctive goodness, but that's just not the way it is.

I was in the second grade when our bus began to make an additional pickup immediately before it took the turn east onto Meadow Road. Several Saunders children had once used it as a stop, but they were older now, and rode a different bus. But since the fall, a thin, quiet little girl had climbed on there. She wasn't in my class, so I didn't know her name, but she was a stranger, she was scared, and she wasn't one of us. So we teased her without mercy.

One night after school, I told my mother how horrible this new girl was.

"Why is she so terrible?"

"She comes from Plainville."

"Well, you've been to Plainville. Lots of times. What's so awful about Plainville?"

"But she comes to OUR school."

"Do you know why?"

"I don't know. Somebody in her family is sick. Her mother or something."

"So, she's staying with relatives?"

"Yeah. Her cousins, I think. But she's terrible."

"Terrible. Why is she terrible?"

There was a pause.

"You know what she does? She brings her sandwiches wrapped up in old bread papers. It's disgusting." It was one of the things we taunted her about.

"Maybe her cousins can't afford to buy waxed paper for her sandwiches. Maybe they're poor."

I pictured the undersized, pale child who boarded the bus each morning in her worn clothes.

"She's poor."

"So, this poor girl has to be away from her family because somebody, maybe her mother, is sick. She could be scared about that. She doesn't know anybody here, and has to go to a strange school. And you kids are mean to her because she comes from Plainville, she's poor, and she has no waxed paper to wrap her sandwiches in."

I was silent. I sure hadn't thought about it like that.

"Did you ever try to be nice to her?"

I shook my head, horror struck. "Everybody hates her...."

"Well, I don't know. It's hard to be the only one to be nice to somebody nobody likes. Of course, she must feel awful."

We were quiet for a while, and I watched my mother sewing the tie back on my school dress. In those days, girls wore dresses to school, and nearly all of mine (and all of everybody else's, for that matter) seemed to be made with a tie on each side at the waist that was meant to meet in a bow in the back. My ties always seemed to be ripped, and I sometimes returned home with one missing altogether.

"I can't tell you what to do," my mother said. "Of course, you get back what you give out. Did you ever hear that?"

I shook my head.

"What goes around comes around. You reap what you sow. These are all ways of saying that the kinds of things you do to others, happen to you. Well, I need to press this off."

It was cold the next day as I sat on the bus rubbing frost off the window with my new, blue and red mitten. I thought about having to go to a strange school, being poor, having your mother sick. When we got to the poor girl's stop, she climbed on, head bent, and went to a seat by herself, as unobtrusively as possible.

I got up and went and sat with her.

"Hi," I said. "Do you live in Plainville?"

She stared at me, nodding dumbly.

"How come you're here?"

"I got to stay with my aunt. My mother's sick."

"Oh."

I don't remember what else we talked about, but this girl was obviously astonished and delighted to be spoken to as a friend. By lunch time, I had told several other girls about her, and we sat with her to eat our lunch. She was wildly relieved and absurdly grateful. Within a few days, other children were talking to her as well, and eventually the teasing stopped.

That winter afternoon, our Sunday School Christmas party was to be held. After school, we walked down the street to the church basement. As we filed into the hall, someone divided us up so that girls went in on one side of the door, and the boys the other. As we entered in our separated lines, a boy stationed on each side of the door assigned a number to each of us.

"Seven," the boy on my side of the door told me as I went in.

"Seven yourself, you old toad," I told him under my breath.

I had no idea why he'd said "seven" at me.

We were provided with something warm to drink and some cookies, and there must have been games. A prayer was said and quiet requested. There was an announcement that a doll and a sled would be the raffle prizes for girls and boys. I had no idea what a raffle might be, but the doll was a beauty. The large baby kind, she was sweet-faced and winsome, and dressed in an old fashioned batiste bonnet and dress, with delicate lace trimming.

A child was chosen to pick a slip of paper from a bowl.

"First, for the doll for the girls," Father Dignan called out.

The child reached into the bowl and handed him a slip of paper. He opened it.

"Seven!" he called out.

I sat.

"Number seven," he repeated, scanning the faces of the girls.

I had no idea the number had anything to do with me.

"Who has number seven?"

Still I sat. I really didn't understand what was going on.

"When you girls came in the door," Father Dignan explained, "a boy at the door told everyone a number. To whom did he say the number seven?"

Oh. I got it now. I raised my hand.

"Well, come up here, Arlene."

I stumbled to the stage. The beautiful doll was placed into my arms. "It's yours," Father Dignan told me. "You won it. You were number seven."

When my father picked me up, it was dark and it was snowing. I raced to the car. "Daddy! Daddy! I won the doll!" He rejoiced with me, and marveled at the doll. She was lovely, and I could hardly wait until we got home. My mother was not there, but was expected momentarily. I crept through to the darkened living room and placed the doll in my own little chair by the fireplace. Then I crept out again.

Almost at once, my mother was home, and it was clear right away that she had known there was to be a party and a raffle.

"How was the Christmas party?" she called to me.

"OK."

"Who won the doll?"

"I don't know. Some girl."

"You don't know who?"

"I don't really know her name."

She walked through the house, turning on lights as she went. She came to the living room and pulled the chain on the lamp by my father's chair.

"OH!" Her hands flew to her face. She laughed out loud.

We hugged, and then we laughed together.

"Oh, you!" she cried.

I named the doll Jacqueline, after a good friend. And when my own daughter neared seven, I told her the story of the poor girl from Plainville, and how I won the doll. And on the morning of my daughter's seventh birthday, Jacqueline waited in the chair by the fireplace.

She shows her age now, Jacqueline. But she is still a beautiful doll, and today she is stored away in a friend's attic, waiting. Maybe someday there will be another little girl in the family, who, as she nears seven, will hear the story about the poor little girl from Plainville, and how at the Christmas party, her grandmother won a doll.

Perhaps there will be a day, when that child grows older, when she will become acquainted with Shakespeare's Hamlet. And perhaps she will do as I did and fall in love with the moody Dane. But I hope that she will know instinctively as I did that when he speaks of the good men do being interred with their bones, the sweet prince is wrong. How could that possibly be true, when the very first "good" I can ever remember doing, is returned to me that same day, wide-eyed and winsome, covered in lace and soft batiste, and I name her Jacqueline.*

Jacqueline now belongs to Arlene's granddaughter Violet.

21. Clyde and the Purple Ink

I was in the fifth grade when Clyde moved to Farmington. Handicapped by what other children saw as an unfortunate name, by ears that protruded at 90 degree angles, and by a distinct Massachusetts accent, Clyde's acceptance proved difficult. It was this last that marked him most. For it proclaimed for all the world that he had committed the most unpardonable sin of all—he had come from Someplace Else.

Kindness to strangers who are peers is not often what children do best. By this time, fifth grade, I was old enough not to overtly engage in the unmerciful teasing this youngster endured, but I do remember loathing him quietly. He was a year behind me in class, but he traveled to and from school on the same bus, and it was there that, for some reason forever a mystery, Clyde began to tease me.

My parents had taught me early that to ignore this treatment resulted in its perpetrator losing interest, and up until that moment, this tactic had always worked perfectly. With Clyde, however, it didn't work at all. Nothing did. He would start as soon as I mounted the bus in the schoolyard: regaling everyone with tales of what he had seen me doing with the most repulsive boy in the school, name calling, and generating particularly disgusting noises which he attributed to me. Each day the situation became more acute, and I had no idea what to do.

In class, for more than a year, we had been practicing cursive writing with stick pens dipped in inkwells. Traditional blue-black ink was provided for this exercise, but it wasn't long before we participants made the discovery of the products of the Carter Ink Company. These marvelous square bottles, available for a dime, soon colored our lives. My friend, Margery, favored green, but my absolute passion became indelible purple.

This magical hue wrote out in a steady Victorian mauve, calling to mind somehow hoop skirts and parasols, but the liquid itself, borne by me in its bright cube with the sturdy purple top, flashed iridescently as it moved, with the unexpected and delightful swirls of orange or green or peacock. I loved it, and I carried it everywhere.

One damp afternoon, I boarded the bus after school to find Clyde waiting for me. He began at once. Noisier and more loathsome that day than ever, my embarrassment knew no bounds. And still I had no idea what to do.

Clyde's stop was some half mile before my own, and I drew breath and settled down to bear the torture as best I could until then. But he accelerated. He became even louder and more gross, and I even more speechless with horror.

The bus swung around to his stop, and without knowing why I did it or what I would do, I got out of my seat and stepped up to face him. This act and the one that followed surprised me as much as they did everyone else. I had no idea what I was going to do until I did it.

With a flick of thumb, I spun off the top to the ink and took it in my other hand. Then I poured the entire contents of a practically new bottle of Carter's Indelible Purple ink over Clyde's head.

For a second or two, he stood, his face, his glasses, those remarkable ears, all streaked with iridescent purple. Then he bolted down the bus steps, and while the other kids roared with astonished laughter, I regained my seat, more amazed than anyone.

My mother met me at our door. In the few minutes to my stop, Clyde's mother had already been on the phone.

Poor Clyde! He was having so much difficulty in this new school. So much teasing, no friends, and now this. Why had I chosen to do such a terrible thing?

I told my mother why. She returned Clyde's mother's call and told her. She offered to have Clyde's raincoat cleaned, and I said I was sorry. His mother said the raincoat couldn't be cleaned. My mother said she was sorry, but offered no new one.

From then on, Clyde avoided me, and I knew peace. In time, he was assimilated and accepted. And eventually he grew into a respected member of the community. Long after I had grown and left the area, I heard that he ran his own engineering company.

I don't know that there is any particular lesson to be learned by all this. Except for me, possibly the meaning of the word "unpremeditated." What Clyde learned, I can't say. Possibly something about the fate of petty tyrants. Certainly something about Carter's Purple ink.

22. The Basement Door

There are moments in history when everything hangs for a moment suspended, just before some spectacular event causes everything to swerve suddenly, careening down an unforeseen bypass, disconnecting us from the previously traveled freeway forever.

So it is that a sailor stands on board the battleship Arizona. It is Sunday morning, and he is peering into the distance at specks in the sky that could be approaching aircraft.

Or the Kennedy's wave, as the open presidential limousine moves toward the coolness of an overpass tunnel in Dallas, a bouquet of blood-red roses on the seat between them. Then in a few moments, everything changes, and will never be the same again.

There are similar moments in personal lives. Some momentous times roar at us unstoppably, generating enormous external change. But there are others, far less outwardly observable, that cause internal changes so profound that the protagonist emerges from the incident different forever after.

I was in the sixth grade when I ripped the door from the Girls' Room "basement." The idea of "basement" was used here as a particular euphemism, since this facility stood on the second floor amid the four "core" classrooms where the fifth and sixth grades, sequestered from the rest of the school, shuttled for class.

The "basement" was a long, narrow room, tiled, and on the left lined with four or five metal cubicles painted maroon and containing toilets. On the right were several sinks, a radiator and a mirror or two. It was a noisy, happy place which we shared with no other grades but our two, and no sex but our own.

We used it to cavort, share gossip, examine our faces in the mirror, and malign boys, as well as a place to "go to the basement."

The doors of the cubicles possessed a latch, but when this was not employed, they swung freely in both directions. It was this somewhat unique factor that occasioned one of our favorite girls' room activities. One chose an empty cubicle, backed the door to its inmost position and ran, grabbing the door firmly and with hands reversed over one's head. Then the girl ran as fast as possible to the farthest outward position and leapt, bending knees back and pressing feet flat against the bottom of the door. Now it was possible to swing back and forth, preferably shouting to one's friends in that deliciously echoing chamber, while momentum lasted.

One lunchtime, when the place was crowded, I was engaged in this particularly exuberant activity. I was bellowing to friends above the din, full of myself, when without the slightest warning the door hinges tore from their supporting structure, and the door itself, with me aboard, flew across the room and hit Joyce Wilson in the head.

It took some confused minutes to ascertain that, not only was Joyce not dead, but also that she did not seem seriously hurt. Once this danger had run its course, and the door lay on the floor and out of harm's way, the flavor of the situation began to shift. The pure terror of having been responsible for such an unforeseen but never-the-less heinous iniquity began to settle upon me, along with the rather queasy but distinct feeling of being a pariah.

Certainly none of us knew what repercussions the situation would engender, but none of us doubted for a minute that they would be dire. This was no minor infraction of the rules. This was a virtual "ripping asunder" of the fabric of our days. I was to blame, and I was terrified. From the vista of years, it might seem foolish, but there have been few times in my adult life when I have been as frightened as I was that day.

"What are you gonna do?" swirled around me, hissing off those tiled walls.

I didn't know what to do.

"I don't know. I have to think. I'm going out."

Into the hall and down the stairs, I inadvertently led a solemn procession of girls, all speculating in hushed tones. Passionately, I wished I were anyone else on earth at that moment.

In those years, the schoolyard of Noah Wallace School was large and seemed to us huge. It contained cement areas directly behind, where one could skip rope and play hop scotch. Steps led up to wide and well-worn fields. There were a couple of scruffy baseball diamonds, and then the fields sloped up in a gentle hill. The rest was surrounded by woods in which we were expressly forbidden to play, and in which we played all the time. It was a marvelous place for children, and we knew every inch.

At that moment, I felt compelled, for some reason, to tread the absolute perimeter of the entire space. My sepulchral entourage trailed, and I tried to think. Could I try to get away with it? Everyone knew who had done it; there seemed no hope of secrecy. Even with the childhood code of "hanging together," and even if no one "squealed," I visualized members of an impossibly large class, assembled and silent, feet flat on floor, hands on desks. Miss Phelon, or maybe even Mr. Robbins himself, went up one aisle and down the next, questioning everyone:

"Did you do it?"

"Do you know who did?"

In the midst of this terrible tension, it would be only a matter of time until someone cracked. Or worse, no one cracked. And, while consequences too dire even to imagine were proclaimed if the culprit were not brought forward at once, the dreadful questioning would begin all over again.

Up one side of the playground and across the top I went. Down the other, and I knew I could not survive that scene, being the felon. Past the tennis court and stopping for a drink at the fountain—my mouth was dry—and back to the cement. Here I stopped and watched a game of "pinkie," and thought how many carefree times in the good old days I had thrown that small, sweetly-smelling rubber ball at the ledge running around the school. If it bounced and you caught it, you could continue your turn; trying for a hit on the ledge when the ball flew up, and if you caught the fly, produced a point. Ah! Those were the days, thought I.

I paused. Now I understood that there was just one thing to do, and I knew what it was. I would have to confess.

Climbing the steep stairs to the second floor, I might have been mounting to the guillotine. The math room and Miss Phelon were directly to the left at the top of the stairs. It was a corner room, big and sunny and filled with those marvelous old desks consisting of curled iron sides and slat for seats. The seat was attached to the desk behind, and I wandered among them now, to plant myself before Miss Edith Phelon—tall, with a gray bun, indomitable. Fair in her dealings, she brooked no nonsense and tolerated no fools. She turned reluctantly aside now from her conversation with another teacher.

"Yes?"

"Um. I need to tell you something."

"Yes."

"Well. See, I was in the girl's basement."

"Yes."

"And, um. I was sort of leaning against one of the doors to the compartments."

"I see."

I gulped. "Well, it's kind of loose."

She pinned me with her direct gaze. "How loose is it?"

I blinked hard, sucked air, and pulled the last of my courage up from somewhere near my feet. "It's lying on the floor."

There was a sudden flash of humor behind the round glasses, a twitch at the corner of the mouth.

"Well, go down to the cellar and tell the janitor," she said, and she turned back to her colleague and her conversation.

For a minute, I stood stuck to the floor. Then I turned and I bolted. I ended up spending a large part of the afternoon in the real basement, next to the glowing furnace waiting for the janitor, and I received a terrible tongue lashing from Miss Phelon when I finally surfaced. Need I have stayed all afternoon? I didn't care. I didn't feel it. I had faced squarely the stone wall of the most difficult dilemma of my life, and had seen it crumble before my eyes.

Of course, what I didn't know then was that the dilemmas continue. But I learned that day about the wellsprings of strength in a moment of crisis, and their power. And I learned not to swing on basement doors.

23. Kangaroo

When British sailors first reached Australia, so the story goes, they were astonished by the peculiar jumping marsupials they saw in such variety, and inquired of the natives as to what they might be called.

The natives of that country, having at that point no experience with the English language, replied politely with their word that meant, I am terribly sorry, but I don't know what you are saying. The word was "Kangaroo."

As frequently happens now, when I was a child, winter clothing often went on sale after Christmas. My mother liked to take advantage of this, and the year I was eight or nine, she took me into West Hartford in January to look for a new coat.

I remember standing in the maroon hound's-tooth she chose, looking with faint distaste at the too-long sleeves and hem, always necessary if an only child was to "get two good years" out of such a major purchase. I felt otherwise noncommital about the coat, but my mother was pleased, and we set out to enjoy the rest of the time until my father would return to pick us up.

It was then that, in a little shop near the clothing store, I saw the kangaroo. It was hand knit of brown and tan wool, and the smiling mother carried her tiny "Joey" in her knit pouch. Not yet too old for a collection of stuffed animals, I fell passionately in love with the kangaroo. My mother told me that she hadn't enough money left for it today, but my birthday was coming, and we would need to return to West Hartford in two weeks to collect the coat, which needed alterations. If the little animal was still there then, I could have it.

It's possible for children to be extremely single-minded, and during the next weeks, I thought often and hard about that kangaroo. I told my friends. I wished. I prayed. When the day finally came, we took the bus in, and I ran all the way from it to the shop. The shelf in the back of the store was full of items as it had been before, but alas, the kangaroo was gone.

I appealed to my mother who appealed to the shop woman. Had they, by any chance, put the kangaroo somewhere else? The shop woman remembered me, and she was very sorry indeed. Not long after I had seen it, some man had bought the kangaroo for his little girl.

I was devastated. Crushed. Until that moment, I hadn't known how very much I wanted that kangaroo. I wanted nothing else for my birthday.

Maybe sometime there would be another one, my mother told me.

At breakfast on the morning of my birthday, I commented politely on the large, illustrated story book, and reached, somewhat listlessly, for the other package. I still thought about the kangaroo.

And then the paper came away, and I was speechless. I scarcely dared touch the brown and tan knitted wool. But how could it be?

My father laughed down at me.

"Who do you think," he asked, "the man was who bought it for his little girl?"

24. Teachers

Bad teachers, good teachers, as I look back, they are all there, along with plenty of mediocre teachers for whom the profession meant a paycheck, and who came and went leaving little in their wake but a sense of lost opportunity.

But of the good ones, the Mrs. Helenes, the Miss Phelons, the Miss Garrisons (she left to join the WACS), three stand out. In their vastly different ways (and good teachers are different from each other, and a good school recognizes and encourages their different styles), each in his or her own way was marked with that indefinable gift that makes a good teacher. Each possessed a spark of magic.

Mr. Gibson taught general science in the Noah Wallace Junior High School. Short of stature, but solidly built, he moved with agility and some grace, and often acted out the tales he told of World War II, when he served in the Pacific theater. Only after the fact did we appreciate the scientific principle involved in particular stories. As kids do, we loved to feel we were "getting away with something," and often word went out before class to "get him talking about the war."

But "Gibby Gabby" had unusual ways to explain what he taught, and flew around the room setting up contraptions, or leaped onto his desk holding a yardstick which he aimed into the sink explaining the science of shooting a skunk in a garbage can. This inevitably occurred just as the principal, Mr. Robbins, with whom he was reputed not to see eye to eye, walked through the door.

He was fully capable of becoming a little crazy with us when a pregnant preying mantis fairly exploded with young, filling her tank with what seemed never-ending offspring. And he used unusual teamwork methods: pairing us up boy-girl, carefully separating current romances, and choosing the pairs himself. Then we worked in teams, conferring on research, writing reports together, and actually consulting each other during tests.

Today, I remain fascinated by many areas of science, and enjoy reading or viewing almost anything on the subject.

Later, I took some advanced courses that left me with little knowledge of the subject, and often with a bad taste in my mouth. I credit both my continuing interest and almost any science knowledge I possess today to the animated and infectious excitement Mr. Gibson found in his subject, and his unusual ways of presenting it.

Our principal, Mr. Robbins, must have stood six feet four, and his silver hair and fiercely strict demeanor inspired terror in the entire school. I think this may have been intentional, I'm not sure, but it certainly seems uncalled for by today's standards.

But Mr. Robbins also taught the ninth graders algebra, and by the time one had risen through the school to this exalted status, we were his pets, and we were safe. There were people in our class to whose grandparents Mr. Robbins had taught algebra, and there was nothing he didn't know about the subject, or about us.

But I was not a mathematically gifted student. I found the subject boring, and successfully avoided understanding anything whatever about it during the first eight years of my primary school career. In those days, before the new math, it really was a dull study, and I would draw lines on the math paper, and during the requisite period, create stories and poems. Then I would take home the work, be unable to do it, give up, and then the next day do the same thing all over again. Mr. Robbins changed all that. He taught the day's lesson for the first ten or fifteen minutes of the class, drawing pictures of it all over the board. He told us what mistakes we would make, and we took positions at the board. Then we were given our exercises and roared ahead, only to hear his deep chuckle behind us, and know we'd been drawn yet again into his trap. In the first two weeks, I'd learned all the math that had been avoided previously, and I understood it, and was challenged and excited by the whole idea. We did our "homework" there at the board, never took a book home, and covered a year and a half of the traditional two years of algebra, all the way through logarithms, in that one year. When, the following year, I took the second year of algebra, the whole first half was a repeat. And I remained awake to the possibilities of the excitement of numbers, and math was never a problem to me again.

In the fourth grade, I hit it lucky. I had Miss Ludwigson. She was tall and blond, and she wore the required suits, high heels and structure of the era with the dignity of a Scandinavian princess. Each child's individuality seemed to wake in her a genuine sense of wonder, and she treated us all with dignity and respect.

If she ever deviated from the approved system, we never knew it, but she had the ability to rise above the mundane. The dull stories in our vapid social studies books she retold in her own words, bringing the people to life. In that racially restricted time and place (Farmington then contained no black or Asian families, and only one Jewish family), we studied George Washington Carver. She informed us that some people said Negroes were not as smart as other people, but look, couldn't we see from this story that a person's skin color was only just that? Compelled to teach us from an agonizingly dull music program, she teased, cajoled and laughed at us until every child learned to read music.

She made us feel valued. When I composed my first novel during that fourth grade year, an opus about a girl who lost her ring in an inkwell, she allowed me to read successive chapters to the class, and praised my prowess. Yet these "talents" excused me from nothing. When I got nine out of a possible eleven wrong on a long division quiz, she insisted I take the second bus home rather than the first, and kept me working until one by one, I got them all right.

She inspired me. When I was taken out of school early one afternoon to see a friend graduate from college, she informed me that "We expect to see you do that someday."

And she appreciated us. When I drew lines over my math paper as usual and began a story, she stopped by my desk as she circulated to check our math word problems. She asked me what I was going.

"I'm writing a story about a knight."

"That's fine, but right now, you need to be doing these problems."

I must have been inordinately naive for a fourth grader, but I seriously believed that the people mentioned in the math word problems were real.

"I've decided not to," I told her. "I've decided that people should solve their own problems. I've got enough of my own."

She gave a quick snort of hastily covered laughter. "Arlene, these are not real people. The people who write these books make up the problems so that children like you can get practice solving the kinds of problems you will have in real life."

"Oh."

"So put away the knight story for now, and practice these other people's problems so you'll be better able to solve your own."

I remember watching Miss Ludwigson, Mrs. Helene, Miss Phelon, and other teachers shivering on the playground in their heels, stockings and dress coats, and thinking, "If I ever get to be a teacher, 1'm going to wear warm clothes out and play with the kids."

I have, and I do.

But if today I am free to wear old jeans, if I choose, and to climb the hills surrounding my school with my students while we all look for dragons, if I am able to let my charges set their own pace and create the curriculum for each as needs indicate, if I am free to experiment, to make my own schedule, and to hug, I do know that Miss Ludwigson is one of the big reasons that I am in a classroom today. Though she wore suits and heels and stockings and never bucked the system. She transformed it.

25. Luck and the Firemen's Jamboree

My childhood was not idyllic. My parents were quite ill-suited to each other, and my mother's sadness and disillusionment created tension and quarrels, and some genuinely bad moments. Nor at that time, did most parents have access to help in understanding either child development or their own complicated and, in my parent's cases, impoverished backgrounds. Children are, at the best of times, fragile and vulnerable, and being a child is of its very nature fraught with difficulty.

And yet looking back, I feel a richness in having parents who genuinely cared. I felt the solidness of life in the same house with the same parents in the same town. If my parents sometimes didn't "do it correctly," if they often focused on me too intently, still they really did seem to like who I was, they appreciated my creativity, and they often found me quite amusing.

They also occasionally thought me clever. And unlike some children, whom accidents stalk, who are repeatedly "caught" misbehaving, or who never win anything, I fell repeatedly without being hurt. I could be naughty and get away with it, and luck followed me like a bright cloud.

Each year in July, the firemen in Farmington roped off a section of Main Street, in front of the town hall, and conducted a fund raiser known even today as the Firemen's Jamboree.

Someone had constructed a number of white and red wheels studded with nails and marked with numerals. These were vertically mounted over booths on which were marked the same numbers as the wheels. People played by placing dimes on the booth numbers, and won if the wheel stopped on that numeral. Prizes included stuffed animals in one booth, donated kitchen appliances in another, and my favorite, the money booth. Here the winner was presented with a dollar.

At the start of the evening each year, my parents handed me a dollar, and told me to come back when that ran out. My friend Paul's parents gave him five. (Paul was also an only child, but as easily tricked and unlucky as I was wily and blessed.) Paul would be seen whining at his parent's side for more funds, while my goal, to end the evening with any stuffed animal I wanted, eat all the junk I chose, and return home with at least five dollars, was something I always managed to bring off.

It was really quite easy. You just went up to a booth and quietly watched the play for ten or fifteen minutes. It didn't take long to discover that some numbers came up frequently, while the wheel never stopped on others. I was never sure why this was true, but I suspect that the wheels may have been homemade, and therefore somewhat inherently unstable. But it was true, and the canny and patient youngster who was willing to wait and see which numbers came up and which did not, only had to choose a favored numeral that had not surfaced for awhile, in order to have favorable odds for winning. The money booth was my specialty, and nearly every other time I played, I won. (This continued to work until the year I became cocky and began to tell other people how to win, and got chased away.)

But I won at other booths too, and although by the time I'd reached my teens the spot of the carnival had been moved, and the wheels replaced with ones I couldn't calculate, those initial experiences have stayed with me. From them, I've gained the profound feeling that "luck" happens more often than not to those who are willing to spend some time learning how the game works, and then watch for the odds before putting down their dime.

26. Girl Scouts

We, my friends and I, were the first First Class Girl Scouts in Farmington. It meant a lot of work and a lot of badges; many notebooks full of activities were completed, and we were proud.

But it meant something else, too. It meant that the guiding hand had been an encouraging but gentle one. In our case, it belonged to Tempi, Mrs. F., who seemed to understand and remain untroubled by our ceaseless need to shriek with laughter over things an adult would find anything but funny. If it annoyed her, she never let on.

I can remember golden winter afternoons at her house, sewing or weaving or gluing or cooking. I remember picnics on Farmington Mountain, and s'mores, and ghost stories around a campfire. And I remember meetings in the local community hall when we climbed out windows, raced around the second floor, or hammered without mercy at the piano.

I remember, too, one spring evening, when Siddy arrived for Scouts with a hypodermic needle she had taken from the trash of a neighboring doctor. She and Margi and I locked ourselves in the bathroom, and chased each other screaming around that small space for the whole meeting. Tempi checked us once or twice and let us be. I have no idea why we needed to do this, what developmental need it answered, or why it was so much fun. I have even less of an idea how Tempi knew to let us be, but she did. Children sometimes need time and space to do things that are spontaneous, annoying, boring, or faintly disgusting. Sometimes all of these.

But my childhood seemed blessed with numbers of these people.

There are long memories of daydreaming undisturbed out classroom windows, the smell of school varnish redolent in the background, and no teacher calling me home. There was time to sit and be, while steaming radiators sent the aroma of wet wool rising, and there were summer days spent so frequently diving and twisting in the water that all nasal passages blocked, and with that strange smell of being under water came the sensation of entering another dimension.

So they come down to me, these thoughts, from a time and place now past. And so have we all, our own places and times that have helped to make us who we are. If, like mine, many of the memories are positive, they linger in the mind as the sour-sweet aftertaste of a lemon lollipop lingers on the tongue.

THE DOOR TO THE RAINBOW

Life in a one-room schoolhouse in
New Mexico

ACKNOWLEDGEMENTS

The following stories, poems or activities are mentioned in this story:

"Duck Subtraction," or "The Whale Game," from Mathematics Their Way, *Mary Baratta-Lorton, Addison Wesley Publishing Co., Menlo Park, California, Reading, Massachusetts, London, Amsterdam, Don Mills, Ontario, Sydney.*

"Miss Viola Swamp," from Miss Nelson is Missing, *Harry Allard, James Marshall, Scholastic Books, Inc., New York, Toronto, London, Auckland, Sydney.*

"An Old House in Paris," etc., from Madeline, *Ludwig Bemelmans, Penguin Books, Ltd., Harmondsworth, England. First published by Simon & Schuster, 1939. Published by the Viking Press, 1958.*

"The Tiger," William Blake, 1794.

"The Eagle," Alfred, Lord Tennyson.

The events described in this story took place during the academic year 1988-89, at the Children's Workshop, a small private primary school in the town of Cerrillos, New Mexico. The school accepts children aged four to eight, grades Pre-K through Two. The events actually happened, and the children are real. Everything attributed to an individual child was actually said by that child, but not always in the circumstances described, as some condensation was necessary to the story.

Arlene C. Walsh

Chapter 1

This morning, I'm ready for the mountains. Some days when I get out of the car at the top of the hill, and go to twist the combination on the lock and swing the gate open, they catch me. The curved hills surrounding this place have sun highlighting their juniper-spotted slopes, and shadows tucked into their folds. If I'm not prepared, it's when I move back up the hill to the car that they grab me. I'll turn, and the contrast of bright and dark in this clear, New Mexico light will stop me with an indrawn breath so sharp my ribcage hurts.

I've been teaching out here for six weeks now, and clearing out and setting up for two before that, and these hills still hold the power to startle me with their sudden, sharp beauty. Somewhere on the planet, there may be a more dramatic spot for a school, but if there is, I have no idea where that place might be.

I climb back into my car and put it into second to ease down the steep incline that is the drive. In front, I stop and back up to the door. Today, I have only the small water container to carry in, along with the other armloads teachers always seem to cart around, and I prop the door open with a rock and begin to take things down the steps and across the school.

It's a large, bright room, well designed for passive solar reception, with the high-ceilinged south wall primarily glass, and the two or three feet wide bancos that run the circumference of the room filled inside with rocks. The floor is five or six steps below ground level, of painted cement except at the west end, where the banco forms a semicircular stage-like area and is carpeted at both floor and shelf level, and the east end, where the library also has a rug.

At 8:30 a.m., the room is already sunny, and crossing it, I notice that the Lincoln Logs, kept with the other manipulable toys on the carpeted west banco, have been knocked over, and that the container is nearly empty. My arms are still full when I spot the crayon basket on the supply shelf, also nearly empty. This seems peculiar, since I completely filled this basket just yesterday with the contents of a new, and especially large, box of crayons. A considerable number of markers also appear missing.

I set down the water container I bring each day (the larger one I fill and carry in only a couple times a week), and I put down my lunch and the other things in my arms on the north banco, about halfway down the room.

Then I see the Lincoln Logs. They have been built into an elaborate fortification that fills the space between the heavy wooden cupboard where I store matches, paring knives, and other things I don't want the children to be able to reach, and the wall. They have been built up nearly a foot high, and bits of cholla cactus and a domino or two have been incorporated into the structure. There is a curiously pungent, woody smell.

Who could have done this? I think of the three little boys who often use Lincoln Logs in building, but why build way over here, and why stick bits of cholla in it? It makes it impossible to touch, and as soon as I begin to disassemble the thing, I have my finger in mouth, sucking. And anyway, this wasn't here when I left yesterday, and I was the last to leave.

I drag the wooden cupboard away from the wall, and stare in amazement. Nearly the whole area beneath the cupboard has been filled. Here are the missing crayons, perhaps fifty or sixty of them, the markers, and the rest of the Lincoln Logs. They have been carefully worked into a structure of astonishing intricacy, all of it interwoven with bits of cholla, and centered with an attractive and comfortable-looking nest of pink fiberglass insulation.

Baird brings in Alana. She puts down her lunchbox, and they both begin to help me clear out the nest and replace the stolen items. Almost immediately, we are stuck by the cactus, and Baird shows us both how to squeeze out a drop of blood and then suck the spot. Both he and I marvel at the construction.

"What could have done this in a single night?" I ask him. "Probably pack rats," he tells me, as we sort out.

"Is there cholla in it?" Natalie calls from the doorway, where she has appeared with Amanda. "If there's cholla in it, it's definitely pack rats. They do that to protect the nest. They can build a nest in a car engine overnight."

We clear and sweep and wash. By the time the other children have arrived, we're finished. Lea and John climb onto the banco at the end of the room where it's carpeted, and begin to build structures for some small, plastic action figures they have brought from home. Sean, our other boy, is not here today.

The girls, currently in a doll cycle of play, have all arrived with "babies," and retired to the library, where they are in the process of setting up a highly matriarchal social structure, involving at least three generations.

Meanwhile, Amanda has spotted the collage materials set out on the art table, and has drifted back. She is soon joined by Ariel, and they both begin organizing and gluing bits of paper lace and some feathers onto cardboard. They are still discussing the doll game with great animation and some disagreement, using vocabulary well advanced for their five and six respective years. Lizzie, six, appears, setting her doll on a chair beside her. The dissention is soon smoothed over, the game set.

Rena, four, streams down the room from the library. The belt to her dress is already missing, she carries her doll by its hair, and she is shoeless. She drops the "child" onto the floor, and plops into a chair. "Hey!" she cries, reaching for the purple feathers. "Those are neat. Can I have some of those?" Katie, also four, has come in now, and stuffing her cubby with sweater and school bag, settles herself at the table, a smile on her round face, and her doll in her lap.

Alana, not yet five, drifts out of the library. She is carrying her school bag, which she proceeds to dump out onto the floor. It had contained a red marker without a top, several plastic knives and spoons, a small and quite worn eyeless bear, and a piece of corrugated black metal that looks like it might have come from a refrigerator.

"I have to go to the bathroom," she announces, and the group working at the table digests this information. It's Katie who looks up. "I'll go with you," she lisps, and they both trek up the steps together. Since it's generally assumed that the outhouse is in some vague way haunted, or at least somewhat scary, it is most often used by pairs, usually age and sex related. And since no one is ever certain just when the need will arise and she or he will want company, and since what can seem downright frightening alone may be a bit exciting with a partner, the children are often generous about accompanying each other.

There is the sound of a noisy engine outside, and its cessation is followed by a loud popping. "That's the popcorn car," Ariel announces, and in a minute, Cailyn, still four, is in the doorway, wearing a red headband to which has been attached red fur ears, lined with satin. She calls her hellos, and runs down the stairs to join the group.

I show everyone the pack rat nest, now resting on top of the trash in the wastebasket.

The boys have left their game, and Lea has removed his shirt and is scrutinizing himself in the dress-up mirror.

John comes to the table, and finding no chairs left, drags one up from the other table.

"God has no bones," he tells us, settling himself.

"That's because He's dead," Lizzie explains.

"No! God isn't dead, is He, Arlene? He's alive."

I'm considering this when Ariel, always logical, takes up the explanation. "He was dead, but then He came alive again."

Cailyn vigorously nods the red fur-satin ears. "Yeah. He got dead, but came alive again."

John's brow is creased, as, at nearly five, he considers the death of God. "I saw lightning and thought it was a skeleton in the sky," Cailyn says. Alana and Katie have returned from the outhouse and are listening. Katie looks around for another chair so she can make a second collage. "You can't see God," she contributes.

"I can't," says Lizzie, holding her collage at arms length.

"Maybe that's because your eyes are too shy," Alana suggests, also dragging up a chair.

Both Lizzie and Ariel turn to look at her. Lizzie wipes the white-blond hair from her eyes and looks again. Neither appear sure what Alana means. John has come to a decision. "God is alive," he tells us.

"The bad guys maybe shot Him," Lea suggests, coming up. He has just turned four, and bad guys and shooting are a deep concern.

"No." John is emphatic. "God is alive. He's with the sheep."

We all look at him a little vaguely, but that seems as good a place as any to start the day.

Chapter 2

Below me, Logan Airport sank rapidly into Boston Harbor. Buildings and landmarks disappeared; in a minute, there were only the fringes of land and the wrinkled water.

This week, I sat in the extreme rear of the plane, between a concert violinist named Arturo, whom I've met before on my weekly commutes between Boston and New York, and the pilot who will fly this Eastern shuttle on its return lap from New York.

The pilot and I have been discussing the date. Exactly eighty years before, December 17, 1903, the Wright Brothers had taken their first "Flyer" aloft at Kitty Hawk. The pilot thought he would make an announcement to that effect on his flight back.

I look past the violinist toward the coastline of New England below. It's been a technologically amazing eighty years. Without this development, my cosmopolitan life style, split between the Back Bay brownstone apartment with its fruit-and-beribboned pressed metal ceiling and elaborate yellow-tiled fireplace, and the ten-room, Upper East Side co-op, would be impossible.

There had been weeks when I took the train, but usually I caught the two subways and bus to the shuttle, and bus and subway at the other end, which I followed with a seven-block walk. Then on Monday morning, I reversed the process. There had been occasions when the pressure of time had necessitated cabs at both ends, but since this tended to double the cost, I left it for more or less emergency situations.

I have always loved to fly, but seldom made this trip without wondering what Wilbur and Orville would have thought of the world they helped to create.

As we pulled up to the gate in New York, I lifted my bag from the overhead rack, hitched it onto my shoulder, and stood waiting as the plane emptied. On the trek through the long corridors of La Guardia, the bus ride past the close-packed houses and winter-bleak cemetaries of Long Island, the standing-room-only subway ride, and the windy walk down Lexington Avenue and up East 72nd Street, I thought once more of my life style.

    At the entrance to my building, the uniformed doorman greeted me by name, and I crossed the thick oriental carpets and polished marble of the foyer. Shooting upwards in the elevator, it occurred to me to wonder, yet again, exactly what I was doing here.

    At heart, I was a country girl. Back in the days before the post-World War II suburban spread, the center of our quiet Connecticut village slid quickly into open country. It was there, in the wooded acres of a state sanctuary that had once included all the wildlife native to the state, that I had spent my childhood. My own children had been raised in a spreading New England farmhouse, also on a preserved track of land, on the edge of a similar town to the north of Boston. I liked the excitement and vitality of the city, and two cities doubled the available art shows, concerts, and poetry readings. But there seemed to be a compulsion among our friends to see all the current movies, to have read and be eager to discuss the absolute latest fiction and non-fiction. I taught, wrote, kept track of nearly-grown children, ran windsprints on the Esplanade in Boston and in the Park in New York, and I commuted. Like many of my friends, I seemed to feel that the important thing was to exude activity, be busy, keep moving. Have you seen the Monet in Boston? TheManet in New York? Heard the Carmen at the Met? Galway Kinnel read in Cambridge? On vacation, where did you go? Where did your children go? Where are you going to go? What are your children planning to do next? Much of the entertaining that took place happened at large cocktail parties where these were the topics of discussion, and where no one ever seemed to sit down.

Two and a half years had gone by this way, and still I kept moving. Gradually, the superficiality of much of the socializing, and dissatisfaction with a failing marriage, had begun to weigh upon me. Certainly I was not the first, and would not be the last, to drink from the full cup and find it bitter. Surely, in the long-past summer nights of my childhood, when my family sat on the front porch talking, while the strains of "Glowworm" drifted down the road from Eleanor Hyde's accordian, and the fireflies seemed to blink with pleasure, surely this was not the rich, full, grown-up life I had fantasized. Was it?

And then spring opened the trees in Central Park and the Boston Public Gardens. My friend Ginny told me that she planned to spend the summer in Santa Fe, and she asked me to visit.

Enough years ago that it seemed to have happened to another person, I had passed through the mountain-cupped city at the end of the chain of the Rockies, and been moved by the pink adobe buildings, the sparkling air, the vibrant quality of the light, and by the mountains.

There had even been a moment, late on a golden summer afternoon, when there occurred one of those flashes that cross the horizon of the mind briefly, lie buried for years, then flash again to change a life. I remember thinking, "Someday I want to live here."

I told Ginny yes. I'd like to visit. Yes. I told her I would go.

Chapter 3

Route 14 south from Santa Fe sweeps down past the infamous Santa Fe Penitentiary, through easy rolling "flatlands," with mountains pulsing at the edge. Gradually the land changes, and changes again. Here crescent, spiked-top rock formations rise like partially-buried stegosauri. Spotting them, one wouldn't be surprised to see a spiked tail emerge from the earth at one end, and a placid-eyed head on its serpent neck from the other.

Here, too, the people of the prairie have come to live. A few native New Mexicans, many more from somewhere else, most are here because they have deliberately chosen a simpler, more basic way to live, close to the land. It is these people, who, some fifteen years ago, set a small, alternative school down beside an arroyo, about halfway between the villages of Cerrillos and Madrid. Some twenty-five miles south of the capital city, the road runs up through the hills, and the school sits below it, to the east.

For three years, I have been teaching in schools in Santa Fe. Now, the one-room school I first visited the year I moved from Boston had agreed to take me on. There will be ten children, Pre-Kindergarten to Grade Two.

One evening in August, there is a general meeting, at which parents, the former teacher and I, due to an extraordinarily wet summer, wildly slap mosquitos. This unusual New Mexican occupation distracts us all, while the children race through the dusk and hover in the doorway, pointing and giggling at the new teacher.

There are the two weeks I spend discovering and sorting materials, dusting and shelving books, cleaning and arranging the room. I plan and organize the school day. There are the last days of vacation, and then we are ready to go.

The first days of school are always a time of assessment. Sometimes the teacher is involved in learning about the children, but always they are sizing her up, feeling their way. During this honeymoon period, the daily schedule is set out, the rules articulated. Next follows a period of "testing," during which the children push against the limits in order to convince themselves absolutely of their existence. Then, if the teacher is lucky, everybody settles down, and the children begin to teach each other and her. Occasionally, the teacher may find a moment when things go the other way. Usually what I have tried to do is to set up an environment as rich as possible, attempt to keep it reasonably safe for everyone, and stand back and watch.

In New Mexico, the autumns are long and golden; the last days of August and first of September still have their summer warmth.

We play in the many "clubhouses" under the juniper, find shady areas beneath rock overhangs to picnic, and we walk in the arroyo.

I am finding out about families. John describes his older brothers, from whom he experiences, according to his telling, severe mistreatment. They are, after all, older, and they do tease.

"How many big brothers do you have, John?" I ask him.

"Twenty," he tells me. It is already clear John loves exactness, loves to put a number to everything. It is also clear that the number of older brothers feels like twenty.

"I had a little sister, too, Katie. But she died."

"That's too bad."

"Yeah. But we got another baby, Bubbles. Bubbles is nice."

We are walking in the arroyo, and the children take turns pulling a long string of red yarn, looped at one end to go around the neck of the "baby girl stegosaurus" we have discovered, and are in the process of leading back to the school. It is Lizzie's turn with the string when she notices that the loop has fallen out.

"Oh, no! We've lost the baby girl stegosaurus!"

Everyone stops and scatters to look, but before we are able to recover her, this utterly real activity is lost in the next spontaneous game.

Sean has killed four of the tigers that have been stalking us, and one after the other has been dispatched with sound effects of loud automatic weapons, and vast amounts of spittle.

Lea, I soon discover, has the climbing ability of a young mountain goat, and is able to remain the vanguard of the group, while scrambling up and down the sides of the arroyo armed with sticks of varying sizes.

It's hot now, and we trail back to the cool of the school for lunch. We wash hands in the water I set out at a raised sink area at the east of the room, and are starting on our sandwiches when Rena lets out a shriek that sends me to my feet. She must have pinched a finger in her lunchbox, or put a chair leg down on a sandaled foot. But when I reach her, she is staring down at her pink and green shorts, and her little-girl legs.

"Oh, my God!" she screams. "Look! I've got chubby legs."

All the little girls, also in shorts, look down, and they wail too. "Look! Look at mine!"

"Oh, no. I've got chubby legs too! We all got chubby legs!" moans Rena's older sister, Ariel.

Maybe it's perfect Barbie, who, never having to apply the back of her shapely legs to a chair bottom, has set the standard. In any case, all the girls seem as disconcerted as the boys seem unconcerned.

Carolann comes in to collect John. He usually leaves after lunch, so he can spend a quiet afternoon preparing for the onslaught of the twenty brothers. She is trailed by the dead sister, Katie. No Bubbles.

They leave, and each child takes a pillow and blanket to his or her own nook, to prepare for "quiet time." After I've swept, the three older children will read and do writing and spelling with me while the younger children continue to rest.

A stillness settles. There is the murmur of children reading or pretending to read to themselves. There are only the sounds of the broom and the buzz of flies in the sunny afternoon.

The hills behind the school rise abruptly several hundred feet. They are flecked with juniper, and, near the top, covered with loose shale. Some of the gradients are steeper than others, and we have walked down the arroyo and climbed from the south, where the angle of hill is gentler.

It is generally considered that we are going to the top of the world, and even on this easier side, the climb is a difficult one. Several of the children elect not to go the whole way, but stop under a juniper, a short distance from the top.

By the time we crest the summit, Lea and John are mere dots in the distance, moving quickly, and heading for a far off bend of Gold Mine Road. It takes some running and shouting to get them back, and then we all stand surveying the world below.

The mountains across are vivid, the road a ribbon.

The children spot my car, and Rena calls out, "Hey, look at Arlene's car!"

"How will I fit inside?" I ask.

"I don't know!" she laughs.

"But look at the school." Alana has noticed its relative size. "How can we get inside?"

"It's a magic hill," Rena tells us. "When you go up, things get little, and when you come down, they get big again."

Lea and John have both noticed this phenomenon, and they find this explanation especially satisfactory. It is Ariel who disagrees, and Lizzie who, as we discuss it later, helps us come to agreement.

"It happens all the time when you go up high or far away," Lizzie explains.

"They look littler, but they don't actually get littler," Ariel tells us. John, Lea, and Rena exchange glances.

"It looked like everything got littler," John remembered.

So I walk part of the way up the drive with Alana, who later can testify to my remaining the same size. The children watch me become smaller.

"Did I get littler?" I ask Lana. "Nope."

Rena is still not certain. "I think maybe all these hills got magic," she declares.

I'm not sure this calls for any disagreement at all.

Chapter 4

"My arms and legs are loose," John tells me, trotting alongside. "From too much exercise."

We are on our way to the river, walking the arroyo the mile and a half to the Galisteo. He has made the observation last week when we held our own Olympics, running, jumping and shooting baskets in the schoolyard until all the children were garlanded with indiscriminate gold-, silver-, and bronze-colored "medals."

"That's because you had all those races," I tell him, but he's off ahead, running with Lea.

In a wide and rock-free part of the arroyo, we had stopped while Lizzie "organzined" foot races, during which there were many winners and much cheating. In vain had I tried to warn that there was still a way to go to the river, and then we had to return.

"There used to be dinosaurs here," John tells me. "In the long, long, long, very extremely far ago times."

"Yes. That's right, John. In the time that was called 'The Age of Dinosaurs'."

"Yes. Right here, in this very spot. In 'The Age of Dinosaurs.' In 1947." We march under the overpass beneath the road bellowing: "Trolls, everything off our bridge." Still the children run ahead, and the day grows warmer.

They are under the fence and across the squishy mud to the water before me. The water is no more than four or five inches at the deepest, and that only in a few small spots. The red mud oozes around the flowing water. It slows me more with my adult size, and I find keeping up with the group no easy job. And although I've been able to round them up briefly on the bank to eat popcorn from a large plastic bag, they are soon off again, and by the time we must start back, much coercion is needed. But finally we're heading south up the arroyo, and now the large plastic bag is heavy with sopping clothes.

Going back, the scene changes. We're only a few hundred yards up the arroyo when Amada wishes aloud that we were back. Now warm has changed to hot, the children lag, and I'm ahead, urging, holding hands, singing. I have little accompaniment. I cajole, they droop.

We chug on. Katie's red cheeks bounce, and she plods, uncomplaining, beside me. Lea, flushed and red, now trails everyone. This is so unusual that I'm not surprised later when he sleeps all afternoon, or when the next day, he has come down with something. His coordination is generally Olympian, his energy boundless.

We are quiet now, no races, no singing, just one foot in front of the other, and all the questions are of how far we have to go still. The trolls are quieter under the bridge, hardly a threat to wayfarers above. Then there's the last fence to wiggle under, the last "cave" of rocks where we sometimes come for lunch, then down and around and up.

Almost gratefully, the children go to their resting places. Lea is asleep at once.

"It was too far," Alana decides.

"But the river was fun," I say. "Got us cool."

"It wasn't too far to the river," Amanda explains. "It was the way back that was too far."

Rae, Lea's little sister, is two, has tiny braids all over her head, and moves as though powered by supercharged batteries.

Today, she tumbles out of the car and races toward the school. "Hi, Suzanne!" she screams, spotting me, roaring ahead.

"That's Arlene, not Suzanne," Lea tells her. But her teacher is Suzanne, so it is her name for all teachers.

She whips inside and pours herself along the top of the banco, in among the manipulable toys. She grabs a "baby" by the arm, trips over the beads, and stops at the blocks, which she begins to empty. By the time her mother is ready to leave a few minutes later, she has demanded and received a cup of water, completed a painting, and appropriated someone else's stuffed elf. When Siri has finished talking to me and aimed Rae toward the door, she is again on the run. Halfway up the steps, she bellows over her shoulder, "Bye, Suzanne!"

Sean has brought his mousse. It sprays out of the handle of his styling brush, and everyone is in the library, amazed and slickhaired. They help each other arrange the latest mod styles.

"You gotta see this." Sean peers around the corner of the library shelf and beckons.

Rena, Cailyn, and Alana have arranged antenna-like extensions to their hair, so they look not so much like rock stars, as invaders from an alien planet. They are well pleased, Sean most of all.

Rena and Alana are fussing at each other. I always have mixed feelings when this happens, since when these two cupcakes are best friends, trouble is usually afoot. The hairstyling has, on occasion and under their direction, run to scissors.

"Rena sticked out her tongue to me!" Alana wails.

"I was just licking my lips."

"No, you weren't!"

"Yes, I was! Hey! There's a little squirrel in my extra clothes." And Rena points to the row of plastic bags hanging on nails from the loft railing.

I'm in time to see a chipmunk streak across the library banco and disappear into a hole to the outside.

Rena dumps her extra clothes onto the floor and picks up her spare trousers.

"Look! He ate the bottom out of my pants!"

There is indeed a chewed-out portion in the rear of her yellow sweat pants. She begins to laugh, her wide-open raucous laugh, and we all join her. It is becoming clear that something will have to be done about the rodent problem.

We are playing in the juniper. The children have cleared out places in the evergreen clumps around the school, thereby creating numerous "clubhouses." Several dolls are stuck into the branches, a plastic bag stuffed with doll clothes hangs from a limb, and there is a collection of used plastic containers in "the kitchen."

At the moment, the play is a mix of domestic and fairy tale.

"We been in this wicked stepmother's house a year already," complains Alana.

On the path below, John and Lea gallop imaginary horses.

"You're always the baby. I never get to be the baby," Ariel tells Lizzie.

Amanda cooks supper in an old pot on a piece of lumber onto which circles have been drawn to represent burners. Below us, we hear the sound of boy-engines. The horses have become motorcycles.

"I'm going to escape," Rena stage whispers, backing up out of the wicked stepmother's house. She stumbles, and I reach toward her, but it's too late. She sits down abruptly, directly into a prickly pear cactus.

This is one of the most painful cacti to encounter, the sting from its needles lasting long after they are removed. Rena's wails reverberate, and all play is suspended as we trail inside, and I remove the needles one by one and try to comfort her. Ariel and Lizzie both huddle close, touching her until the sobs subside.

Now tales of who else has fallen afoul of a cactus commence, and is followed in due course by those of who has come eye to eye with a rattlesnake. This is rattlesnake country, and the story is told of how, when Lizzie's older sister, Josie, was here at school, Gavin, who was teacher then, killed one in the schoolyard. Climbing as we do all over these hills and rocks, I am perpetually uneasy concerning possible encounters with rattlers.

In my lap, Rena is quiet, and she soon slips down and play is resumed inside.

I look south. This wall of glass reveals that the sky, glittering and bright only a while before, is sullenly overcast, thick with high, gray clouds. I call to Rena.

"Look what's happened to this day," I tell her. "The whole sky was clear."

Rena is in the process of descending the steps near the entrance. Halfway down, she sits, and with her little square knees spread, her dark green dress dropping between them, she raises her wide-spaced eyes, nearly as green as her dress, to the ceiling, and her lusty baritone fills the school:

"Oh, you my sunshine,

My beautiful, beautiful sunshine.

Make me happy when skies are gray.

Oh, my sunshine, come back, come back,

I love you dear sun,

Please don't take my sunshine away."

Lunch is over, and I'm sweeping the floor. The children are playing Billy Goat Gruff on and under the larger of the two classroom tables. They organize themselves, arranging various turns as billy goats and trolls. As is often true, they don't need my help, but are able to communicate complicated directions, and to take turns in ways that seem fair to all.

Pete arrives to collect John, and Johnny points out the large sheet of shoe rubbings that hangs in the window.

"Those are our shoe reflections," he tells his dad, as they pause to look. "See, Sean got a dinosaur on the bottom of his."

Rena trots by me, carrying a pillow and a doll. "Look," I say, pointing out the window.

"What?"

The sky is now completely clear, vibrant, New Mexico noon blue. "Look what you did. The sun is back."

She stands a moment, contemplating all that blue. Then she grunts with satisfaction, and trots off to her resting place under the library loft. It is only what she expected she could do–no more, no less.

Chapter 5

Lily is a red sheep. At least the tip of her wool is reddish, then gray, and close to the skin, white. It has a silky, cobweb-like quality, and spins into a soft mottled color, gray-white flecked with red.

Lily and a goat named Alice had been loaned to us at the school where I taught last year; and when, at one point, Lily escaped, she outran dogs for three miles, crossed the busiest intersection in Santa Fe at rush hour, and ended up in someone's yard stamping her foot. What can you say about such a sheep! By the time the school year had come to an end, I had fallen quite in love with this long-legged, mixed blood New Mexican sheep, and when the owner agreed to sell, I bought.

But I live in town, in the old residential section, so where can I keep Lily? Then my friend, Karl, tells me about a friend of his who lives on the pueblo in Nambe, and who has just acquired three sheep. I call her, and she is enthusiastic about boarding Lily.

We take Lily up to Roberta's, and, as we bring her into the sheep pen, the three sheep watch with interest. For Ramsay, the wether, it is love at first sight. He reminds me of the old cartoons, where, on seeing the girl, hearts come out of the boy's eyes. But when we leave, and I twist in my seat to see that striped face watching the car go down the drive, seemingly saying, "You're going to leave me here with these strangers?," I feel like a parent walking away from a child on the first day of school.

That night, Lily refuses to sleep in the shed with the other sheep, and instead goes to the farthest corner of the pen and lies down. When Roberta goes to check on them later, the other sheep have left their shelter and gone to lie in that remote corner of the pen beside Lily.

By the next time I visit her, however, my call of "Lily, Lily, Lily" brings her not to me, but sets her running off, looking over her shoulder. It is clear that she wants me to understand that though she may be glad to see me, the company of others of her kind, the rich alfalfa hay, cracked corn, sweet oats, and all the outer leaves of spinach and lettuce that Roberta brings from the restaurant where she works, plus the affection Roberta and her ten-year-old daughter, Povi, lavish on these animals, have won her soul. Lily has always been clever. She knows sheep heaven when she finds it.

Today, we are on a "field trip" ("Arlene, when are we going to get to the field?") to the sheep. We've been looking forward to it, talking about how mammals work in general, and sheep in particular.

The hills and mountains zig-zag in the distance all around Roberta's place, and the children tumble out of the cars and race toward the sheep pen. Amanda, small and delicate, seems a bit timid about the proximity of large animals, and lags, but the others pour inside as soon as Roberta has the gate open. Povi helps us catch Lily, who stands resignedly, as she is hugged, petted, and liberally addressed in baby talk. They circle her, feeling the wool, sticking their fingers all the way in to feel the skin beneath. Lizzie leans her cheek against the red wool, and there is a faraway look in her eyes. Alana puts her nose almost on Lily's and crosses her eyes.

"Wooga, wooga, wooga, Lily," she says.

Lily stares at Lana, then rolls her eyes sideways. The ends of her sheep mouth stretch up, she adjusts her weight, and seems to drift off, a faraway look in her eyes, too.

Later, while carrying lunch boxes, that we spurt under the back fence and trail along an old path to a monstrous cottonwood. This is a cool spot for lunch, and the children eat a little, drink a lot. Roberta has thoughtfully provided extra drinks, as it's warm for early November. Then Alana's mom, Busy, Roberta, and I sit under the tree watching, while the youngsters climb nearby rocks.

Lea is at the top almost at once, then Ariel, who comes down almost at once, to help someone else up. Then up and down they go, mountain climbers, Indians, wild game hunters, explorers, until it's time to leave.

The afternoon light is clear and yellow and fills the car on the way home. The three boys are full of animal questions, stories of their own prowess, displays of bipeds. As we crest the hill before the spot where the road to Cerrillos Center cuts off to the right, we spot a cyclist, who has dismounted and paused beside his bicycle at the top of the hill. He stands gazing with a rapt look east, to where the mountains rise and fall in the bright air. His head is tilted, his clipped beard accentuating his air of appreciation. He holds the bike and gazes smiling into the distance.

"Look!" cries John as we sail past. "There's Odysseus!"

I think of the Greek tales with water-color illustrations that are so popular at school.

"Well," I tell him, "it sure looks like Odysseus."

"No, Arlene, it doesn't look like Odysseus, it IS Odysseus. It's Odysseus and his bike."

Autumn in New Mexico is long and golden, and the weather holds, from our sheep visit early in the month, to our trip to the Albuquerque Zoo just before Thanksgiving.

Katie's mom, Luann, drives this time, and walks the zoo paths with us. The lion is showing off, roaring and raging, with pauses to assess the effect on onlookers, the giraffes rock along watching us, and an ostrich tries to nibble heads, hands, and hair over its fence.

The tiger sleeps in the sun. The children race up and break at once into choruses of "Tiger, tiger, burning bright," shouted and spontaneous. We watch a moment or two, while, flat and immobile, the tiger moves nothing, not a whisker, not the tip of its tail—nothing.

Alana shrugs. "He's used to it," she says. "He knows he's the tiger." Several rhinoceroses stand rippling their thick skin, leering at us with their beady eyes.

John races up and grabs the fence. "Hey!" he shouts. "There's a triceratops!"

I hate to diminish his fervor, but ask him to count the horns.

"Oh, it's not triceratops. It has only one horn. What is it, Arlene?" I suggest rhinoceros.

"Or," says John, thinking, "maybe proceratops."

I take in the thick, dun-colored skin, the sense of force, of power, and the mean eyes. "Close," I think to myself. "It's got to be close."

Luann and I sit by the pond after lunch, and the children squirt each other with the fountain, jump off the benches, and run on the grass.

She asks if I am going home for Thanksgiving, and I tell her no, I'm going to visit my friend, Gail, who lives near San Francisco, and whom I met when we were both in nursery school and four years old. It was at Mrs. Jenner's Nursery and Kindergarten, in Farmington, Connecticut, and she is not only a cherished friend, but also someone with whom I share memories that go back to the source. I watch these children racing by the water, and it's the little things I remember, things that mean nothing to anyone but us, yet come unbidden, soft and small and sweet, like the hairs on the back of a baby's neck.

Someday, some part of these days may move with these children into their future. I hope it may nourish them as my memories do me.

"Well, then," says Luann, "you are going home."

"Yes," I tell her. "I guess I am."

Chapter 6

The weather stays warm this year, on into December, and without a storm or even a killing frost the flowers still bloom as the Christmas holidays approach.

I clang the triangle that hangs by the window outside the front of school, and the children appear from the juniper clumps, sifting inside and toward the east end of the room. They form a kind of line at the raised sink area, waiting, as they do, to wash for lunch.

Flies still circle the lunch table, a disadvantage of no frost, with me whomping at them, feeling this must be what the Australian outback is like in hot weather. The children are sharing bits of their lunch with our new kitten. She is completely black, not a speck of white anywhere, and this, coupled with the fact that all signs of any rodents have disappeared in the week she's been with us, has occasioned her name, Midnight Magic.

The children are deep in discussion of who wants to be what when they're grown.

Cailyn puts down the spoon to her tofu. "A swan!" she cries. "And a mermaid. I want to be a mermaid who takes care of little mermaids."

Katie is chewing her sandwich, a dreamy look in her eyes. "I don't know," she says. " I don't know what I want to be."

"Me neither." Ariel crunches her chips. "I think I'm too young to decide. And anyhow, Arlene, what I don't understand is this. About *Sleeping Beauty*. Everything is asleep for one hundred years, right? Even the dogs and cats. Even the flies on the walls. Right?"

"That's how I know the story."

"Then, if the whole palace, and everything in it is covered with cobwebs, how come spiders get to stay awake to make the webs?"

"A blue Superman!" Lea calls, his mouth full of apple. "I'm going to be a blue Superman when I get big."

"A princess!" Rena shouts. "I'm a princess."

"Yeah. A princess." It sounds good to Alana. "I'll take care of animals."

"How come!" Ariel prompts. "Arlene. About the spiders."

"I haven't any idea, Ariel. And anyhow, you're the only person in the world who would ask me that question." Ariel returns to her place at the table with a little smile on her face, pleased with herself.

"I'll be a ballerina," Amanda nods, pointing her toe and fluttering her arm. "I'll dance."

Rena agrees. "Yeah. Me too. A belly dancer. Right now I got a belly dancing suit at my home." Her pronounciation of ballet is interesting.

"I like ballet," Alana informs us. Amanda nods. "Me, too."

"We did *The Nutcracker* before," Ariel remembers. "But it was too much. We had to wait for hours and stay up till about midnight."

"Yeah. *The Nutcracker* is too much," Lizzie agrees. "What do you want to be when you grow up, Johnny?"

I am still swatting at the flies that are everywhere. Cailyn pokes a dead one with a finger.

"Don't! Don't touch that!" John is emphatic. "Doncha know flies got poopy hands?"

Cailyn is surprised. "They do?"

"No! Johnny," says Elizabeth, "what do you want to be when you grow up?"

Suddenly John is sure. He slaps his hand down on his empty lunch bag, and shoots it toward the basket. He misses. Lea does the same thing, and he misses too. Lea gets up and picks them both up, dropping them into the basket. "Thirteen!" calls John. "I'm going to be thirteen."

We are at the carpeted end of the room in group time, discussing our Christmas pageant. The children will depict ways of celebrating Christmas and other festivals of light around the world.

"Look!" Sean cries, pointing. "A tiger!"

We all turn and look through the glass wall to the hillside beyond. "Not a tiger," says Lizzie.

"Two! Look!" Lana shouts.

There are two, and they're not tigers. "Wolves!" Sean decides.

"No," says Amanda. "No wolves here. They're coyotes."

They are indeed coyotes. A pair, the color of the earth, loping diagonally up the hillside. We all run to jump onto the banco, leaning against the windows.

"I know they're wolves!" Sean is emphatic.

"Not really, Sean. Just good old coyotes. A pair of them." I tell him. "Wow," John breathes, his hands on the glass, his face pressed close. "Not wolves," Lea murmurs.

"A pair of coyotes," says Lizzie. They disappear to the north.

We jump down and drift back to the circle. "That's amazing," I tell myself and the children.

"We saw coyotes," says Lea.

"Yeah," echoes Rena. "But we just got to see it happen. We didn't get to tape it."

There are low clouds and the smell of snow in the air the day I borrow my friend Ginny's jeep, and John's mom, Carolann, and I get set to take the children into town on a surprise field trip.

"Why won't you tell us where we're going," Ariel wheedles. Lana tugs my dress. "Yes. Why?"

"It's a surprise. But I think you'll like it."

At the larger of the two Santa Fe malls, a new double-decker carousel has been constructed. It's dotted with mirrors, gleaming all over in brass and garlanded with lights.

"Tell us," begs Lizzie, leaning against me.

"If you don't tell us, I'm going to explode. Really." Rena's eyes are wide, and she has drawn herself up as tall as she can, and is holding her breath, looking explosive.

She lets out her breath. "Waagh! You're a mean teacher."

"What can I tell you? You have a mean teacher."

Katie takes my hand and jumps up and down. "Tell us! Tell us!"

"You'll just have to wait to find out." Loud choruses of "aaaghs," as we head to the cars. Dust of snow is blowing across the road as we start into town.

"It's in town, isn't it?"

"How much farther?"

"Are we almost there?"

"Not too far, now. It's my Christmas present to you, and I hope you'll have fun."

We pull up to the big doors of the mall. "It is the mall!"

"The Violinda Mall!" (The Via Linda Mall.)

"I knew it was the mall."

Then we are inside.

Cailyn's hands fly to her face. For a moment, she and the others are frozen in place. "Oh!" she breathes. "Oh!" There is just the momentary pause as the glitz hits them, then they are running, off and around, to the entrance. "You may each have two rides, so pick two things that you want to ride on...."

"The Cinderella coach!" "The white horse!" "The upstairs swing!" "The black stallion, two times!" We ride and we ride, into fantasy.

Natalie has met us there with Amanda, and she buys the children huge, flat M&M cookies, which we don't expect them to finish. They do.

There's a long run down a long hall to the bathroom, and a slow walk back to the cars.

"I could have went on that a hundred times. Two hundred."

"A million thousand."

"But then we wouldn't get back in time for the party tonight."

It's dark as we gather in the hollow by the arroyo. The children have come into the other building (once used for another class) to put on costumes, while the parents mill about in the school.

Lizzie's a Lucia with a wreath to which candles have been fastened; Rena, in a red dress, gives out coins and candies wrapped in red paper (as the Chinese are reported to do at the New Year); Sean and Lea are piñatas; and Amanda and Katie, as firolitos (our southwestern lanterns made of paper bags containing sand and a candle), are inside large paper bags in which arm and leg holes have been cut. Alana holds a menorah to celebrate Hanukkah, and Ariel is a candle. John wears a green cloak to which ornaments have been pinned, and is a Christmas tree. A glittery star is tied to his head with string, and the star is at an alarming angle.

We assemble at the back door, and one by one the children walk the length of the room as each representation of some festival is read.

There are the suitable "oohs" for the elegantly dressed girls, a general chuckle at the dragon piñata, and a roar of delight at the "bagged" firolitos. The "twenty brothers" appear to have some difficulty masking what looks like a collective desire to fall onto the floor and roll around screaming with laughter, as the Christmas tree with the lopsided star staggers down the room to take its place at the stage area of the room.

It helps when we sing carols, and after that the piles of food are uncovered in the dim light. We eat and talk, the groups shifting, the children becoming increasingly wild as they pour along the tops of the bancos, chasing Midnight and each other.

The teacher is presented with a card containing a collected donation, and Sean beckons me aside and pulls me down to his level.

"There's real money in there." It's a stage whisper. "You can buy stuff with it."

I'm grateful for the information and for the gift, and we begin to scoop the trash together and sift outside under the prairie stars. Out here, the stars don't just lie along the top of the sky, like the- cover on a casserole dish; the whole sky itself bends, and comes down all around us, all the way to the earth.

Tonight it stays like that all the way home.

Chapter 7

It is winter now in New Mexico. There are occasional snowstorms, with slippery mornings and the sun out soon after. There is the short light, the frozen earth.

The children and I pull in, sit close, hang together.

My days start now with stoking the stove, stuffing it with paper, splitting the kindling to go on top, bringing in armloads of wood. A friend gives me an axe, and I split and bang and smash, while children hold their ears.

The building has been so well placed and designed that the passive solar heating is terrific, and when the sun is out (and that is most of the time), by noon, the room is a greenhouse. The children end up changed into summer clothes. Sometimes the girls will strip down to a slip. These have become increasingly popular since Christmas, and are always worn with four or five inches showing below the dress. If you can't see it, why wear it?

After a snowstorm, it's sometimes difficult to know whether to have school or not, since where I live in town, tucked in under the mountains, conditions are often quite different from what has happened out on the prairie. The small lanes and side streets in my neighborhood are often left unattended and can be dangerous. Sometimes I worry, and complain about the driving.

Alana comes to me and motions me aside. Her voice is conspiratorial, concerned.

"Arlene, do you have forward drive?"

"Oh, yes," I am able to tell her. "I go almost nowhere backwards."

"Oh, phew!" Her relief is obvious, and I have been able to ease her mind without any need for prevaricating concerning four-wheel drive.

Some days we walk in the arroyo. There are often fresh coyote tracks, always jack rabbit, and sometimes things we can't identify. When Sean finds the prints of tigers, the boys will always follow them, racing ahead. Rena trails, one end of her scarf dragging in the snow. Her conversation is vivid with what she has noticed. The air is almost crystalline now, sharp and bright, like breathing seltzer.

One day, Sean has a tantrum. I will not let him bring a long and dangerously pointed stick inside, and as the children say, he "loses it," shrieking and raging, while I sit on the steps holding him. I clasp him firmly as he lashes out, and I tell him it's a grown-up's job to see that children don't hurt themselves or anyone else. I say I will let him go as soon as he calms down. He screeches that I'm choking him, choking his ribs, and Lizzie comes up and stands for a few moments, watching, and then goes off. One or two other children do too, and then from the corner of my eye, I see Rena and Lana smiling at me, a little too sweetly. They are sitting on the floor near the easel, and they are taking their shoes off.

"I can't breath!" wails Sean. "You're choking me!"

Lana nods in my direction, and I see Rena giggle. They are pulling off their socks.

"Arlene, I can't find my Star story," Ariel says, coming up.

"Let me go! I want to go!"

"As soon as you can be calm, Sean." "I will be calm!" kicking out.

"Look in the publishing box, Ariel." I cling and pat.

"I did."

"Did you have it up in your resting place? Were you working on it there?"

"Help! I'm dying!"

"I don't know. I'll look."

"As soon as you calm down, Sean..."

John and Lea have built an enormous block and leggo construction, and they are flying plastic action figures above it, apparently oblivious to anything else.

"It's not here," calls Ariel from the other side of the room. "Maybe in the loft..." She disappears.

"Aaaagh..." screams Sean.

And then I see Rena and Alana. They are taking sly peeks over their shoulders to see if I notice them. That's when I spot the long, twisted line of paint footprints snaking down and around the room. They've seen me good and busy and have taken their chance. They know there'll be the devil to pay, but it's worth it. How often does the chance present itself to paint your feet blue and walk all over the school?

As the day for the new president to be inaugurated nears, there is much talk of presidents. We have a wall chart with pictures and a book that tells the dates and terms of office of each, as well as a fact or two calculated to interest children. Some interest me. I hadn't known that Dwight Eisenhower was a pilot, that Martin Van Buren gave speeches from table tops because he was so short, or that Calvin Coolidge had a pet raccoon named Rebecca that he walked on a leash while in the White House.

There seems to be a general feeling of relief and appreciation in discovering that the new president must promise to do the best job that he can. "Oh good," says Lizzie. "I'm glad he's at least going to TRY."

The assassinations are of special concern, and there is much discussion and many questions about which presidents met this end.

"But not George Washington. He died of natural causes."

"Alana wasn't alive then, but God was," says Rena.

"What's natural causes?" Lea wants to know.

"Well, as I remember, I think he went out riding in terrible weather and caught a bad cold, and it turned into pneumonia, or something."

"George Washington is DEAD?" screams John. "He's DEAD?"

"One guy got shot in a car," Lizzie tells no one in particular. "I think that was Kennedy."

"And one guy got shot in the movies," calls Rena from across the room.

"Oh, yeah," John nods. "I know that guy. That was Hammershead Linkerson. Arlene, are you sure George Washington is really dead?"

The snow when it comes is always dry, and full of mica-like crystals that glitter and sparkle in the light.

Amanda takes the wide push broom outside and drags it in an almost endless path along the top of the snow. It twists in and out of the juniper, down through and across the arroyo.

All the children follow, trailing out behind, keeping single file in the "path," and singing over and over, "Follow the yellow brick road. Follow the yellow brick road. Follow, follow, follow, follow, follow the yellow brick road."

They do this on and on and on, with no sign of tiring, every time it snows.

I stand in front of the school, watching the trail of children pied-pipering out of sight behind the building, reappearing on the other side. "Follow, follow, follow, follow, follow the yellow brick road," and I clang the triangle reluctantly, to call lunch.

We climb the hill to the road to talk to the telephone people who are putting in a phone line for us. They are digging under the road with a machine they call a "mole," and its steady "thwonk, thwonk," has filled the last few days. We belly down to look at the cord disappearing into the hole, and we stand on the spot in the empty road that is directly above it, and feel the vibrations in our bodies.

Later, we watch the backhoe dig a trench all the way down the drive and over and across to the school. Later still, another telephone worker appears and makes the hook up, and we have a phone!

I am relieved, since no one ever seemed to be able to receive me on the mobile phone, and I feel safer. What would I have done in an emergency? Yet now and again it rings, and that always comes as a kind of shock. The peace feels disturbed when it happens, and now the potential is always there. Now there are calls I feel I need to make from school. So, we now have a line to the outside world, but they also have a line to us. It's safer, and I wanted it, and I'm not sorry. But there's a break in the circle that wasn't there before, and I have to see it, and admit it, because I've always thought of it as going only one way. But each gain brings with it also a loss. It's a surprise, and not what I thought before, but something I've only recently begun to suspect.

It's the quiet time after lunch when everyone takes a break, each child in his or her own spot, while I clean up. The younger ones continue to rest while I work with the older, on writing, spelling, and reading.

But after the holidays, I've started the kindergarten-aged children on writing too, and they puff with pride to come to the table to work on letter strokes with the "big kids." Katie blows her cheeks out and concentrates so hard that the paper under the pencil rips. Cailyn leans over the work, watching, drawing each mark with infinite care, each line, each practice swirl. Rena sits ramrod straight, the cables of her sweater going down her back rather than her front, a fat red pencil in each hand.

Then there's a kind of general exhaling with self-satisfaction as they finish up and each goes back to her own nook. Rena falls asleep. Alana is singing quietly to herself the words that seem to her to go to a book she is "reading."

Going back and forth to the outhouse during rest time, a child will often slip on the old clogs that I keep near the door, and clomp, clomp off in the distance, or slip on my long moonboots that come up to nearly everyone's thighs. They are sounds and sights I get used to, that become a part of this time of day.

Amanda, Lizzie, and Ariel do reading worksheets and take turns reading to each other and to me. Lea turns in his sleep, still clutching a plastic horse John has lent him. Midnight purrs on Lana's mat. The stove crackles softly.

I'm sitting at my working spot, a desk chair, placed so it looks south, just to where the hills to the east and west dip, and I can see rising between them the Ortiz mountain, capped with snow.

We're making valentines. Lace, red paper, tissue, and glitter are everywhere, and Cailyn and Lana have used so much glue, their cards will take a day and a half to dry.

"Our dog died once," Johnny says.

"Oh, yeah. I know somebody who got dead," Lea nods. "I can't remember the name." He chops masses of red paper with the scissors.

"My Grandma died. We had to bury her up," John remembers. Lea digests this information.

"When things die, we bury them," I say, cutting my own valentines.

"If you don't, they get stinky," Lizzie tells us.

"Oh, yeah, I know about that," Ariel nods.

Rena takes a small plastic brush from a large, brown pocketbook, and begins to brush first her doll's hair, and then her own.

"You can come alive again," says Lea, hopefully.

"No, Lea, if you're dead, you stay dead." Lizzie speaks to him seriously. Lea says nothing.

"Our cat we used to have runned away," Katie tells us.

"Yeah, yeah." Cailyn nods agreement. "I remember...." she drifts off, staring out the windows, forgetting what she remembered.

"You know what?" says John. "God is everywhere." He is watching Rena. "Even in your hair."

Chapter 8

There's a splash of rainbow on the door, two on the north wall, and another on the ceiling. The children have been running back and forth for fifteen minutes trying to find the cause, and have yet to spot the various prisms I've hung in the windows. They are difficult to see unless you know just where each is. Cailyn chases the light, putting her hands into the colors. "It's not esposed to be here," she tells herself. Ariel runs outside and peers back in, trying to discover the rainbow source.

At the smaller table, we are making knight helmets out of construction paper.

"Prisms!" shouts Lizzie, arriving and running down the steps. "It's got to be prisms. Look for prisms." Ariel comes back inside, and they search for prisms, but these still prove elusive.

"I can't find my bat car," Lea says, coming up.

"What did you do with it, Lea?"

He regards me with exasperation. "I lost it!"

"I percoove the rainbows, but I can't percoove the prisms," says Amanda.

Alana comes in and drops her lunchbox in the container by the door. She puffs out her hair with her hand, and joins us at the table. "How do you like my puffy hair?" It explodes around her face, rather like the mane around the head of a lion. "I put it in braids."

John considers her. "It looks like you put it in the dryer."

I slip on the knight's helmet I've made and the children watch me. "I found one!" calls Lizzie from the window. "I found a prism!"

Alana is watching me and the knight's helmet. "Now take it off," she says. "I want to see your regular face."

Everyone jumps on the banco to see the prisms. There is some discussion, and a list is made of what you need to make a rainbow.

"Rena has naked socks," laughs Amanda as they jump off.

Rena looks down. "Sometimes I never forget where I put my shoes," she says.

Amanda drifts over to the other table and begins construction on a paper doll that's called a "Heart Bunny," something designed, it seems, to take up the slack between Valentine's Day and Easter. The other girls are soon doing the same.

Cailyn's looks a bit peculiar. She holds it up.

"That's delicurous!" Rena shouts, leaning toward her.

"Don't talk in people's faces, Rena," Cailyn retorts. "It bugs them."

John and Lea have come up and they spread out a large Donald Duck puzzle on the big table.

"When I grow up, I'm not taking drugs," John announces.

"Me neither," Alana agrees.

"Yeah. If you don't take drugs, they give you a dog mask." We all look at him.

"Anyway," Alana droops, "my birthday's all over."

"So what?" Rena tells her. "You'll have a million more."

"Yeah," says Lizzie. "Unless you die."

We are sitting on the floor doing duck subtraction. There are large pieces of thick, white paper in front of us, onto which everyone has arranged ten small duck crackers.

Midnight sits watching with interest, and the new kitten, Blake, comes streaming out from the library end of the room, and skids through three people's duck crackers before she slides to a halt, distracted by a bug near the water cooler.

"Look what Blake did to my crackers! Blake!"

"Blake!"

Blake, a tri-colored tiger, has been named because of the children's favorite poem, "*The Tiger.*"

An unrepentant Blake cocks her head at the insect while we rearrange crackers and distribute new ones where needed.

"Mine got all mooshed."

Crackers once again set, our right hands become whales, sneak out and grab two crackers, which we devour. Then we count, and talk about how many crackers you have left if you start with ten, and a whale eats two. Now a shark appears in the form of our left hands, three more disappear, and again we count. This we've found to be a wonderful way for the younger children to begin learning the number facts zero to ten, and for the older children to start internalizing them.

So we continue, until all the crackers are gone. Then more are passed around, and we start again.

Now Blake loses interest in her bug, and comes skittering sideways back through the crackers.

"Oh, no, not again!"

"Blake!"

Blake grabs one of Katie's crackers, and runs to the other end of the room.

We finish, and the activity is recorded by each child in a green notebook, used for keeping math and pre-math records. And we're ready to go outside.

Cailyn comes up to me, eyes wide. "You know what? There's a song singing inside my head, and it's not even coming out my mouth!"

We drift outside, Blake watching us from the window.

It's after quiet time, and we're at the art table, making purple purses from paper, for "P" day. There's been a lot of "snuggling" today, that is, resting with a partner, so the quiet wasn't really very quiet. It will be awhile before we do that again.

We are talking about things that start with "P." "Penis," Lea figures out. "Boys got a penis."

"That's right, Lea," I tell him. "Penis does start with 'P'. And boys and men do have a penis."

"And girls got a 'china'," Rena explains.

Lana giggles. "Girls got a 'china'."

I correct the pronunciation as matter-of-factly as possible, and there is some more discussion of who has what, as the girls begin to make coins to stuff into the purple purses.

"Planets," muses Ariel, "start with 'P.' Know what I think? The planets are God's flowers, and when He waters them, it rains!"

"Boy! Look at all the money we're making. We're making tons of money!" Katie has already cut out and colored a large pile.

"Wow!" Alana scoops up a mass she has created. "Look at all the money we're making. We're making lots and lots and lots of money!" She thinks for a moment. "We're lawyers!"

All of us have been reading *Miss Nelson is Missing*. This general favorite, concerning a second grade class whose unruly behavior sparks the arrival of Miss Viola Swamp, "the meanest substitute teacher in the whole world," is a topic of conversation.

"She's mean as a bean! Yuck!"

"She's a real witch."

I slip outside, and quickly comb my hair over the front of my face. Then I stick my sunglasses on over the hair and return to class.

I use my best witchy voice. "Heh, heh, heh! Here I am, Miss Viola Swamp, the meanest substitute teacher in the whole world!"

Lea stares.

Lizzie grins, and Ariel roars with laughter.

Katie guffaws, and throws herself at me, nearly knocking Miss Viola Swamp off her feet.

Rena pulls at my dress. "See, you can tell it's Arlene by her dress. See!" And she repeats this several times, convincing herself and anyone else who might need it, before I go back outside, and return as myself.

There's been a trip to Albuquerque to see the Museum of Science, where the most fun of all seemed to be baiting the Tyrannosaurus rex with roars and "nah-nahs" then running in delicious terror when this mechanical monster roared back.

Now Carolann is driving again, as we set out once more for the sheep. Lily's lamb, Bambi, is now a month old, and Roberta's other ewe, Sheeba, has just produced a little black newborn.

"Blah, blah, black sheep, have you any wool," sings Cailyn.

It's a cold, blustery March day, and several of the parents have decided to keep youngsters with runny noses at home, so we're all in Carolann's car together.

"Boy," says John. "It's really terrible."

"What is, John?" I ask him.

"My Granny. She got spiked."

"I'm not sure what that means."

"She took a haircut. She looks terrible."

"Blah, blah, black sheep," sings Cailyn.

It's so cold, that after we take turns to hold and hug the lambs, we eat inside Roberta's trailer.

Natalie meets us there, and Amanda is much less intimidated by the lambs than she was by the sheep, though she still complains about the animal smell of the sheep that most of the rest of us like so well.

After lunch, we walk out to the horseshoe-shaped hills behind Roberta's. Owls live in the cliffs there, and Povi shows us where to find the tiny bones of rodents the owls drop.

The sun comes out weakly, and the children clamor to take off coats.

John finds a cow skeleton, and he enlists help in dragging the larger part of this back to the car. We set this out on the low "exploring" table at school the next day.

Rena puffs in, stomping and blowing. "Boy!" she shouts. "I was sick! I catched yammonia yesterday."

"We missed you," I tell her.

John is studying postcards of New York and San Francisco that have been tacked to the side of a bookcase. "Listen," he says. "Don't go there,

Arlene. You won't like it. It's a dirty mess."

"Where did you get these cow pieces?" Lizzie is turning over John's cow skeleton in her hands.

"Yesterday. Up at Roberta's. John found it."

"It's nice, Johnny."

"Anyhow," says John, pointing to a picture of the Golden Gate Bridge, "I've seen the wires of the city move."

It's the end of the day, and we're gathering for candle time. Annie has come in for Cailyn a bit early, and joined us. We form a small circle around the candle, hold hands, take a deep breath, and close our eyes for a quiet moment. Then we drop hands, open eyes, and take turns telling something we liked about the day.

"Playing in the clubhouse with Lana."

"Playing in the clubhouse with Katie."

"Journal time!" cries Lea, referring to the time each day we spend doing original work in a hardcover 9"x12" book.

"You always say that," Ariel tells him with a grin.

"I like it," says Lea.

"I know you do," I tell him.

"I liked squeezing the love out of Lea," giggles Rena.

Lea beams. He looks at Annie, and begins to count backward from ten, possibly to impress her. (We do a lot of rote counting: by fives, by tens, up and back to twenty.)

"That's great, Lea," she tells him. "Do you know what comes after zero, going backwards?"

Nobody does.

"Below zero, all the numbers are called negative numbers."

"Oh, I get it," Cailyn shouts. "Like at the bank!"

We all turn to her in surprise, and then it's time to blow out the candle and blow out the day.

Chapter 9

We've planted bean plants in plastic cups and watched the roots form. This morning, for the first time, as "the cruelest month" slips around, the last of them have broken the soil.

"Look!" cries Rena, pointing to the cup with her name on it. "My bean plant is hatching!"

Katie wiggles the cup with her young plant in it, now four or five inches high.

"Yours will be a beanstalk soon, Katie," I tell her. "Will you climb up to the sky and see what's up there, when it gets that big?"

"Sure," she grins at me. "As long as you go first."

John, in a red baseball cap that folds his ears down and sideways, lines up plastic bowling pins and rolls the large ball at them. "Wow!" he shouts, knocking them all down. "A hole in one!"

"John lost his rememory," Katie laughs.

"That's not how you call it," says Heather, the new girl who has joined us, since Sean, whose mother needs to work full time, has taken him out and placed him in full-time day care. "You call it your brain."

Johnny heads toward the door, bowling left behind. "I'm going outside, Arlene."

"Stay in front." The children are allowed out when I am not, only if they stay to the south of the building, where I can see them through the windows.

"Come on, Lea," he calls. "Come with me."

Lea looks outside. "It's too drippy out," he decides.

Several other children are working on a classification project at the art table. They are cutting animal pictures from old magazines and gluing them onto mural-sized paper.

Alana has been drawing at the other table. She comes up and presents me with a picture done with markers. Steep sweeps of color form a tight camber. In the arch below is a door.

"It's for you," she says. "It's the door to the rainbow."

"I don't like Johnny. Do you like Johnny?" Rena asks Lizzie.

"I like Johnny."

"But not right this second, right?"

Ariel muses. "Sometimes I feel that way about somebody."

Cailyn comes in. She is wearing sneakers and carrying a pair of party shoes. "I brought these," she laughs, dropping the party shoes on the banco. "In case my feet get bored."

Lea brings a book and stands beside me. "Read this to me." I look at him.

"Please."

"OK."

A group of us head to the carpeted banco and settle to read. Several other children have brought up books, as well as Lea. Alana does not want to wait, so Ariel takes her into the library to read to her.

"This first," says Lea, setting a book on my lap.

"*Madelaine*," mock-reads Katie, "by Alfred Lord Tennyson."

She curls into herself and rolls away from us, helpless with laughter at her own joke.

We read of the "Old house in Paris, covered with vines," and the clock over our head ticks.

We are all playing in the junipers. There has been so much quarreling, such screaming fits, so many bitter tears and frustration today, that we're tired of it.

Lizzie is frying some juniper berries and dirt on a piece of wood. "I think this is one of those days. All the clubhouses except for that," she motions with her head over her shoulder, "are too small. And they won't let us in the big one."

"You can come in mine," Lea calls from next door.

"No, Lea, It's too clautrarodic."

Alana pokes her head in. "Come on. You guys can play with us."

"We don't want to," pouts Ariel. "You keep bossing us. You guys always got to be the boss."

"Arlene can be the big sister who gets punished for riding her motorcycle in the kitchen," Lizzie says, casting me in the family role that seems a favorite.

"I'm going to ride my motorcycle in the kitchen again!"

"She's so BAD," says Rena in delight.

Ariel sits with her knees drawn up under her chin. "This has been a terrible day," she mourns. "Not a single thing has gone right all day. I wish this day was never born. And I hate my lunch."

Rena regards her sister in silence for a minute. Finally she turns her palms up and shrugs. "Well," she says, "there's nothing you can do about it now. You can't unwind life."

We sit chewing on this while the sun turns the drops of water on the juniper tips to diamonds.

It's the day after vacation, and I'm attempting to gather everyone together for group time, and I'm having limited results. Several of the children are up in the closet area that the parents have partitioned off on a Sunday workday, and where the recently donated computer has been set up. They click away.

Alana is seated at the art table, a large pile of recycled paper to her left. She takes a page from the top of the pile, pretends to make quick notations with a pencil, slams that paper down to her right, sighs heavily, and picks up another. She repeats the process again and again.

"Come on," I call to the children at the computer. "We need to have circle."

"We got to finish this game," they call.

"Just <u>that</u> game."

Lana scribbles, slams down paper, sighs. "You, too, Alana."

"I can't."

"We need you now." There is the sound of renewed clicking, the soft, internal beeps and pings of the computer. "Hey! You people! Don't start another game."

"Come on," calls Lizzie. "We're waiting." The cats have already joined us, as usual. The computer operators finish and stream down the stairs to circle. "Lana, we need you."

"I can't," wails Lana, stomping and sighing, "I have to do my taxes."

"Finish them later. We need you now."

She joins us, reluctantly. "My taxes," she moans, "are 499."

We sing songs, and begin to tell what we did on spring vacation.

"Slept over my grandmother's."

"Went to Colorado and visited our friends."

"My cousin came. We had a sleepover many nights."

"My whole family," John tells us, "climbed the tallest mountain in the world. One hundred and six feet. You had to have special equipment, and nails on your shoes."

"My friend Sandy came," I explain. "And we shopped and we walked and we shopped and we walked. We shopped so much, I thought my legs were going to fall off."

"I'm glad they didn't," says Lana, still clutching the pencil she's been using to ward off the IRS. "Then we would really have a short teacher."

Reading time for the older youngsters is over, and our snack this afternoon is a cake in the shape of an "L," for Lea. We frosted it this morning, and are eating it this afternoon. There's been a song for Lea, who will leave next week for Spain, where his family will remain with relatives through July. Lea sits on the table, one leg folded under him, beaming with pleasure. There are some altercations about pieces with the most frosting.

Lizzie is thoughtful, remembering working in her reader. "Boy," she says, thinking what comes next in the primer, the story of an early aviatrix. "I can't wait to read about Amelia Airline."

"I read about her," Ariel remembers. "She flew around the world and got lost."

"They never found her. No one is sure what happened to her. You won't get lost in Spain, will you, Lea?"

Lea laughs and shakes his head.

"Arlene," says John, who has stayed all day today, to help celebrate with Lea. "Do they put ham inside of pigs?" His mouth is full of cake.

"No," Ariel tells him. "I think they take it out of them."

"You mean they got it inside?"

"Sort of. I think so."

I wonder if and how I need to add to this conversation.

"Pigs are confusing," John decides, wiping frosting on his shirt. I determine to leave it at that.

Alana strikes her forehead with the palm of her hand. "God," she exclaims. "I got to finish my taxes."

Johnny and I are sitting on the table, turning the globe. There are questions about who lives where that pile into each other faster than I can answer. The poles are of particular interest, and so is a concern about Santa Claus and who gives him gifts at Christmas.

Alana is being difficult. She has totally disregarded several specific instructions, and done instead the opposite of what was asked.

Rena calls from the library. "Who wants to smell my tummy?" She has several takers.

"It smells good!"

"Yeah!"

"Did you put something on it?"

"Yup." My mommy rubbed some special smelly powder my daddy gived her on it."

"Alana, I need to have you put Blake down now, go get your journal, and do it. Everybody else is finished."

Alana takes Blake and goes to sit in the library.

"Ok, that's it." I go fetch her, take her hand, and lead her to a chair. "You need a time out. Just sit here for awhile."

She flounces down, chin at an angle.

I move to the other table to take dictation for someone's journal story. These are usually creative and interesting, but often long; and there are, as a rule, three or four or even more of them. The ones we like best get copied later, illustrated, and put into a colored folder, by way of "publication."

I glance at Lana. She is sitting now with head bowed, weeping silently. This is only the third "time out" I've had to give to anyone all year. I wonder why this is true. Is it the small number of children? The mix of ages? The absence of the emotionally troubled children present in so many schools, who take such a disproportionate amount of the teacher's time? Is it the other ways we've been able to set up to work things out? Or does the fact that most of the adults these children deal with understand and accept them as the unreasoning, magical, amoral creatures children are until seven or eight? Certainly, it's true that these youngsters are often able to settle difficulties without my help. And it seems true as well, that they care about, and help to take care of, each other.

Later, outside, Lana comes up behind me, and buries her head in my skirt. I reach around behind me to hug her, and we go to sit on the climbing structure, where people are lining up for the rope swing.

I glance at my watch and look again. "It can't be!" It tells an hour beyond where we should be, where I thought we were.

"We ought to have had lunch an hour ago! Aren't you hungry? I've lost a whole hour, and I don't even know where it went!" I stare again at my watch.

Ariel shakes her head. Her attitude is one of benign resignation. "Oh, Arlene," she tells me. "You lose everything!"

Chapter 10

There are no rainbow patches inside now. Because of the building's placement and overhang, no sun has penetrated inside since May has come. We are preparing to leave for the dance which celebrates the feast day of the San Felipe pueblo. These ancient rituals feature dancing off and on all day, by clans or teams dressed in costumes treasured by families. Dancers are meticulously groomed and painted, and the Indians are unfailingly gracious about welcoming visitors.

Amanda and Lizzie each hold one stuffed hand of a child-size Mini Mouse, which Amanda, with her instinctive sense of design, has won in a coloring contest. They are walking her around the school.

Anne, Lizzie's mom, and Natalie, who will be driving, are trying to help me round up people.

Alana is seated at the art table, absently slicing up paper. "My mama says I can't play with scissors at home any more," she says.

John is wetting his hands with water from the water cooler, and standing before the dress-up mirror, slicking down his hair.

"How come, Lana?" I ask, trying to gather up and put away materials.

"'Cause I cut the phone line."

Lizzie and Amanda are still walking Mini.

"When I grow up, I'm only having one child," Amanda decides.

"Yes!" Lizzie knows exactly what she means. "So they won't fight."

"Let's get the show on the road!" I call.

The lunchboxes go into the back of Natalie's car.

"Let's leave before you're all grownups."

"And turn thirty," says Rena.

"That's old," Katie tells her.

"Thirty is not old for a grownup," Lizzie decides. "But it's old for a kid."

"My mother is sixty-five," John informs us. "I think."

Finally, they are all in the cars, and we head up the drive, and south, toward San Felipe.

"My dad was in the first war," John says.

"The First World War?"

"Yes. But he was only thirty at the time."

Katie is in the front seat with me, and ahead of us, we can see Mini's head in the back of Natalie's car, bobbing above the lunchboxes.

"I sure hope Mini doesn't eat all the lunches," Katie giggles.

At the dance, we find a place on the sidelines in the shade. We sit. The group of Indian singers chants to the steady heartbeat of the drum, the dancers in the intricately-embroidered costumes move in and out in the complicated patterns—all under the relentless sun.

The children are most impressed with the Indian youngsters, some as little as two, who, with costumes perfect, and arranged according to height, keep going, patterning themselves on their elders, the twenty or thirty minutes each team continues at a time. There is a mesmerizing quality to it, to sit and feel the drumbeat vibrate through your body, hear the overlay of the chant, the shuffling of the dancers.

I think of the instructions one Indian mother is reported to have given a child about to dance. "Hold your heart high, place your feet well. Then you will be in harmony with all things. Then will the rains come."

We picnic by the river. With great adult encouragement, Cailyn eats a little. As usual, Ariel does not like her lunch.

"I'm not sure I should eat this," says John, showing me. "This applesauce is wrinkled."

On the way home, most of the children sleep.

Now we're practicing daily for our closing ceremonies. We'll sing many of the favorite songs, recite "*The Tiger*," and "*The Eagle*," dance the Maypole.

People drift in later and later now, and by the time we're all present and ready to go, it's hot out.

Each day, as we launch into "He clasps the crag with crooked hands," from "*The Eagle*," the red-tailed hawk who lives on the hill behind invariably appears, circling. Cailyn nearly turns inside out, everyday. "LOOK! There he is!" The other children shout, point.

"It's the red-tailed hawk," I try to tell them, but they are sure.

"No," says John. "That is the eagle. He comes out every day to hear his poem.

There is total agreement among the youngsters, and the creature's arrival each day is so punctual and on cue, that I am completely unable to dissuade them.

The Maypole dance becomes more tangled every day. And it's hot.

"I'm sick of this."

"It's too hot."

"I need a drink."

"Listen," I tell them. "Do you remember how the Indian children danced? Did they complain that it was hot?"

Heads shake.

"Did they whine for a drink?"

"No."

"They just did it."

"So just do it," says Lizzie, and they do. And little by little, day by day, slowly, it begins to come right.

At quiet time, everyone asks to hear *Best Friends for Frances*, every day, as one of the stories. They have learned the small songs Frances sings as the story unwinds, and each time we come to one, children sit or kneel up in their places, and from all over the room, the light, high voices come, joining in.

There are many visits to the outhouse now, especially during rest. Flycatchers have built a nest there, and are busy feeding their young. We can just see the heads and wide beaks over the edge. The children are careful not to go too close—respectful, full of wonder.

Alana has been sounding out word families, rhyming, for weeks. "See we three bee me tree," she chants.

I make some small books of the word families, and one day at quiet time, she rips all the way through "Dan ran to the tan van," etc.

I close the book. "What did you do?"

"What did I do?"

"You just read that."

She stares. "No."

"Truly."

"Truly?"

"Truly."

I hold up the book. "Alana just read this."

From all over the various nooks of the room, where there are resting children, comes quiet applause.

This morning, we've explored the new Children's Museum in Santa Fe, and then my house. Similar methods were used in each place. At the museum, the water troughs were splashed in, climber climbed on, snake followed. At my house, drawers are opened, hats tried on, and if no actual jumping is allowed, much wiggling and pillow tossing takes place on the bed. We eat lunch on the terrace.

Now we're on our way back to school.

Coming into town, I've warned Cailyn, Rena, and John to sit quietly, and not distract the driver. On the return trip, the conversation is relatively quiet.

Cailyn turns to Rena and John. "I think the moon is plastic," she tells them. "Is the moon plastic?"

"I don't know," Rena says.

John holds up a sticky mass. "My gum is rotten. What should I do with it?"

I take it and put it in the trash.

"Gum gets rotten," Rena notes. "Got any more?"

"Nope."

"But is it?"

Rena considers. "I had a pin once of the moon."

"Yes. That's what I saw. It was plastic."

"So I guess the moon is plastic."

"I guess it is."

"Arlene," John wants to know. "Are we abstracting you?"

And then, somehow it's the last day. I have sent out a call for flowers, and because there's been no rain all spring, the parents have told me there are no flowers. But this morning, here they are. Full buckets line the wall, the table is covered with blossoms. Each child chooses, and I put together tape-covered wire wreaths for the girls, a lei-type band, worn crossways on the chest, for Johnny. All the children make up bouquets to be presented to parents as a thank you.

Ariel tries on her wreath. "We're going to be beautiful," she says.

Katie studies the completed wreaths floating in the water table to keep fresh. Each has a name attached.

"They're all different," she notices.

"People are all different," Amanda tells her. She considers. "It's good. If everybody was the same, you couldn't tell who was who. You couldn't tell people apart."

At quiet time, we forego rest and set out to Madrid for ice cream at the Madrid General Store. It's a somewhat subdued group that gathers around the circular table, licking.

"Tonight," someone murmurs.

"Tonight."

"I can't wait."

We finish, pile back into cars, and in a couple of minutes are at school again.

"Boy," says Heather, climbing out of the car. "Ice cream really makes your neck longer."

"Yes!"

"It does!"

There is immediate understanding and agreement.

That evening, as I round the corner on the road above, there are already cars parked at the building, and I experience the familiar jolt of joy as I spot the little school by the arroyo below.

I ease down the drive and pull to a stop to find children running everywhere. Cars are following me down one after the other, and finally we send parents and friends and everyone outside, gather the children together. The flower wreaths are drying on paper towels set out on the table, and are at last bobby-pinned in place. One after the other, youngsters run to the mirror. "Boy, are we beautiful!" Lizzie cries.

"Yes," I tell them. "You are."

It was spitting rain, and now has stopped. Parents wipe off the chairs we've set up, and I warn the crowd that's gathered—I've never seen so many people here—and inside we form first a small circle, hold hands, wish each other luck, and then a line according to height, and we are ready to go.

"I love you all," I stage whisper.

Heather's voice comes back to me down the line, clear and high. "We love you," she says.

The processional is the ancient spring, or May Day, carol, and the children wind through the crowd and mount the climbing structure. Each section of the program is announced by a child, as we sing the songs we've practiced, recite the poems. As we start "*The Eagle,*" they turn to look, and there, sure enough, is the hawk, as ever on cue, circling.

The plain muslin strips we practiced with have been replaced with pastel streamers, and as the Maypole is proclaimed, the sun drops below the navy blue clouds that lie over our heads, and the children are focused in a light so yellow, so thick, so intense, it seems almost ethereal. They take their places, I nod, and the old Shaker song "It's A Gift" rises, acappella, as they weave and turn, turn and weave, flawlessly, in the gold light.

There's the party, the food, in the room with its clothesline full of art; and the children, in their "beautifulest" clothes, come to lean against me. There are the gifts: the flowered dress with lace collar that I might have chosen myself, the earrings in my favorite color.

It's been a year when many of the dreams I've cherished all my time as a teacher have come true: days exploring a genuinely rural setting, numbers small enough to tailor each child's curriculum individually, the safe environment. "It's everybody's school," they tell each other now. And, "Anybody can play."

But all things change. Route 14 is being widened out as far as Lone Butte; they're piping water to Cerrillos. Progress. Next year may bring us flush toilets, possibly a day care facility in the unused building. My feelings are mixed. If I've learned anything this year, it's that every technological gain is a two-sided coin, and the other side of that gain is some kind of a loss. We may have an inside toilet, but no flycatchers will build in the eaves there. Only with care will the magic hold.

Now we're cleaning up, planning to meet at the campout tomorrow.

"See you there."

"Sometime in the afternoon."

Outside, the clouds are gone, and the stars out. Again.

It's over. It's gone.

And not gone. Like the stars, taking their light-years to get to us, we've just started to send out our own light.

Somewhere, small hands still slip into the rainbow colors refracted onto the walls. Somewhere, quiet applause echoes from all corners of a room where a child has just read for the first time. Somewhere, in a light too rich, too golden for mortals, young voices float in an old song, and a Maypole is woven. Sometime things will be different because of what has been, here.

Sometimes you open a door and step right into the rainbow.

THE SKY'S THE LIMIT

How women can realize their dreams
in later years

FOREWORD

You are permitted to read this book at any age. You are required, however, to have a dream.

"Courage is the price that life exacts for granting peace." Amelia Earhart

FROM ANOTHER PLACE

Did you ever look into a mirror and see another face looking back?

It has happened to me. Possibly it connects to my love of flying and its history. I don't know.

It was early morning and I was car camping at the Biplane Fly-In at Bartlesville, Oklahoma. I had forgotten my hand mirror and had moved from the folded-down rear of the car where I sleep when I car camp, to the front seat, where I adjusted the rear-view mirror to put on my lipstick. Then I looked into it.

The face that looked back at me was that of a young man in a World War I flying helmet. The image was black and white and gray like a photograph, and I squinted, focused and stared, but it first faded and then vanished. The mirror was empty. I blinked, looked again, and saw my own face.

Two different people, at different times and places, both who considered themselves psychics, had told me that in some other life I had been a British pilot in World War I, and had been killed in action. I don't believe this, or disbelieve it; who knows about these other dimensions?

Reason tells me that what probably happened was that I'd seen a photograph of a World War I pilot that I didn't consciously remember, and still a little sleepy, had transposed it onto the mirror. Yet I felt sure that the face I had seen had seen me, and that the eyes I had looked into and that had looked back at me, had been my own.

Chapter One

Howard and I sat on the kitchen floor cutting out paper dolls. His long khaki legs were crossed in front of him, and I was splay-legged and a little open-mouthed, because he was telling me what it felt like the first time you killed a guy.

"I thought the whole damn Luftwaffe was after me," he said, cutting out Betty Grable's skirt. "I got outta there as fast as I could. I was never so scared in my life. When I finally got her on the ground and they got me out, I threw up my guts."

It was a madly inappropriate thing to tell a child, and I loved it. I loved hearing the details of his dogfights, and I adored him.

Howard's elder brother Ed, whom we all called Buddy, and his younger brother Raymond were also pilots and also in the war. Ed, because he had two children about my age, was stationed in the States where he trained other pilots, and Ray flew officers, often high-ranking, around the Pacific. My earliest memories included models made of balsa and brightly colored tissue, which they made and launched all over the house.

Now in our kitchen, Howard flew his hand along the air and flipped it smartly upside down to demonstrate how he flipped his P47 Thunderbolt. The time would come when I would actually see him do this on film, but some fifty years would have passed. And only then would I be not only working on my own pilot's license, but also be building my own plane to fly after I got it.

But all that lay far in the future as we sat on the kitchen floor cutting out paper dolls.

Ahead lay years of growing up in a postwar world where gender ruled strictly, and the feminine meant home and motherhood. Rosie the Riveter was gone. She had dissolved into the staid suburban housewife of the nineteen fifties and early nineteen sixties.

Also ahead lay the tumult of the later sixties. Protests for which I was already too old and too tied to a young family, proceeded without me. Black and white assassinations and a war that wasn't, assaulted the senses and unsteadied the psyche. Buried beneath the layers of not only raising a growing family but also of becoming a teacher, moments of special enjoyment sparkled. But I was the one who prepared and executed these. And I was the one who cleaned up afterward.

As a high school project my elder son and two friends studied Wilbur and Orville Wright, sent to the Smithsonian for plans of the 1903 flyer, and over the course of a year in which our lives were filled with bits of the first airplane, built a replica they sold to a west coast air and space museum. During that year we all learned a good deal about the early history of flight, and my interest from an earlier time tingled below the surface. But I remained a combination of roles rather than a person; I knew what I was. I had no idea who I was.

But as I sat with my cousin on the kitchen floor that evening, these things lay far in the future. There was no hint then that when my children had grown and gone, I would come to discover that I was not who I wanted to be. In addition, the crushing sadness of a marriage in which, I felt, my own needs were unacknowledged and unmet, even by me, became unbearable. And so I chose to leave my northeastern roots, and set out for a new life in the Southwest.

There, in a world of mud walls and Byzantine blue skies would I begin to discover my wounds and begin the work of healing them. Only then would the onion layers of persona begin to peel away. I knew I was a teacher, a writer, a mother, and eventually a grandmother. Only slowly did I begin to see at the core someone who wanted desperately to fly.

And what a place I'd chosen for it! At seven thousand feet Santa Fe, New Mexico, lies in a cup of mountains. If I could learn to fly here, I ought to be able to manage it anywhere. Three hundred sunny days a year meant there were a lot of days available. Funds on a teacher's salary meant there were not. It was then I learned the two most important lessons anyone needs to know in order to fly her dream.

First, no one learns anything, to speak a language, to play an instrument, even to walk, all at once. Everything is learned in a series of small steps. Second, the same holds true financially. In the case of an expensive-to-use and complicated flying machine, the steps must also be small. At least it is so for me. Things may not proceed with all the speed to which our fast-lane society has become accustomed, but with priorities and determination they can proceed.

So it was that on a bitter January day I took my first flying lesson. I couldn't remember when I had been so excited. We rolled down the runway and rose into the air. I was level with the mountains and saw the sun below me as we made a rectangle of the field.

"Are you tired? Do you want to quit?' my instructor watched me.

"Are you kidding? I've waited my whole life to do this. I'm never going down."

It feels that way still. Everything took me a long time. Everything was difficult. And every single flight anyone takes is always a challenge. That's part of what it's all about.

I don't now remember where I first heard about the Experimental Aircraft Association. This international group was begun after World War II by Paul Poberenzy, and today has groups, or chapters of people who like to build their own airplanes, all over the world. I do remember receiving a list of the names of people in my local chapter, a combined Santa Fe/Los Alamos group called the Green Chili Chapter. Someone told me where the next meeting would take place, and on a black October night I arrived at the appointed house, and peered in the window. A roomful of mostly men stood about talking with their hands and exhibiting more animation than I was used to seeing anywhere outside the kindergarten. I rang the bell and walked in. It wasn't long before I too was talking flying and nothing but flying. It felt wonderful.

That night began a friendship with people of an organization that has proved unfailingly supportive, helpful, and just plain fun. Nearly all the members have built, refurbished, or are building planes. Sometime during my first months as a member of this group I became aware of the term "home-built," and the germ of an idea was planted.

It was also during my first months with this group that I discovered the joys of fly-ins. These are held regularly at various airfields, and sometimes have a special theme, such as antique planes, and sometimes not. We would fly off in various machines, chattering and joking by radio. If we stopped for breakfast the flying stories continued there. Then we continued to our destination. If you love planes, it's an exciting sight to arrive and see so many airplanes in one place. We spend our days walking the flight line looking at planes, attending workshops, perusing booths full of books about flying, paraphernalia for flying, clothing for flying. We talk to other pilots. Evenings, after dinner in groups together, we spend hours in the motel pool and hot tub, where flying stories continue into the wee hours, and into utter exhaustion.

Sometimes I shared a motel room. Once I slept on a sleeping bag in the corner of a room where three men also slept, and all three of them snored! It was through the EAA as well that I discovered classes in building airframes, and about engines and how they worked. They were taught by an instructor from the Embry School of Aeronautics, and were held at a small airport on the north side of Albuquerque. These proved invaluable to someone who, before beginning flying lessons, had not understood how an internal combustion engine worked.

It is before one of these classes, very early in the morning, that I stand by the hanger where these classes are held, waiting for everyone to arrive, and for things to start. Classmates and I are looking up into a sky still pink with early day, watching another class member enter the pattern to land. There is quiet chatter and easy laughter, and in that gentle moment I know myself closer to the bone of who I really am than I have ever been before.

When my cousin Ed, eldest of the three flying cousins, developed Parkinson's disease in his eighties, his children were helping him and his wife Betty move from their Oregon house to one in northern California, closer to their own. While cleaning out a cupboard they came upon a collection of eight millimeter spools of films labeled "Howard's Fighter Pilot Films." These turned out to be films taken from cameras in the planes Howard had flown in combat. Ed's son Gary transferred them to video, and in due course sent me a copy. There, in the silent, faded Technicolor of a time long gone, I saw Howard flip his P47 Thunderbolt just as I had seen him flip his hand, while sitting on my kitchen floor so long ago.

That young pilot, a member of the Eighth Fighter Command, 82nd Squadron, 78th Fighter Group, was among the first to arrive in England. He led a D-Day squadron, was shot down three times, and to my huge relief, survived the war. He arrived home in June, 1945, and I remember that he still wore his khakis while he tucked me into bed one evening, and told me that he would see me the following Wednesday, when he would come back to go fishing with my father.

On the intervening Saturday he took a small plane up, and set out to fly over a local lake and drop a hat to his uncle, fishing below. No one has ever really understood what happened then.

Only lately have I come to understand a little of what these young pilots had endured: the endless bombing and strafing, the killing that didn't stop, the eventual refusal to make any new friends because they had seen so many close friends killed in so many violent ways. And there was the sometimes unbearable tension of the constant missions. I've come to wonder if, under Howard's happy-go-lucky manner, lay issues not yet resolved between killer and hero, terrorizer and terrorized. Could that have contributed to what happened? Was there a moment when he might have expected the power of the P47? Because something did go terribly wrong, and he flew into the hill at the side of the lake. He was killed instantly. He was twenty five years old.

Arlene's adored cousin Howard on the wing of his P47 Thunderbolt. The picture was taken just before D-Day.

CHAPTER TWO

I guess I should have suspected sooner. There were clues.

Sometimes, in the quiet clouds of an early summer afternoon, a flicker of knowing, sudden and clear as lightning, flashed, and I would understand that somewhere lay hidden the possibility for a kind of fulfilling joy as yet unknown.

Then there was the recurring dream. It is night in this dream, and I climb into the pilot's seat of a small plane. Howard is in the other seat, and we fly off into a feeling of happiness so complete it feels ecstatic.

Still it didn't occur to me what these hints could possibly mean.

But I had grown up in an era when men returning from war had taken back the jobs outside the home, and women were encouraged to complete themselves only through becoming wife and mother. No one would have considered telling a man he would be totally fulfilled only by being husband and father. Instead, men identified themselves with their work, and both sexes remained unbalanced.

During the years when I was a child, nobody I knew was suggesting to girls and women that they create themselves authentically by following their passions. Nobody I knew was telling anyone female that the deep delight of being of service to others could not happen to a non-person. I never heard girls told that being taken for grated in traditional roles might well produce emptiness and bitterness, yet I saw this all around me. To me no one spoke of finding out who I was and becoming that person. No matter how much my friends and I accomplished on our own, the tendency was clear. Women nearly always defined themselves in the reflection of a man, unless, gulp, she didn't "have" a man. And as our families grew, we saw ourselves reflected in our children as well.

When I married and began to raise a family, like most women of my time, I did it single-handedly. At that time most men helped little if at all at home. My job, I was told, was house and children, and more than once I was left to care for them alone when I was too sick to get out of bed.

Nor had I any idea how deeply the culture of the time had permeated the very cells of my being. I saw myself as so many women did then, as daughter, wife, mother. The growing dissatisfaction I found as the years went by deepened into an unhappiness so profound it sat like a lead ball in the center of my stomach.

By the time I finally understood that my sane survival meant setting out on my own, I accepted the portion of what had been mutually attained during the marriage and set out to start again. I even refused generous offers of financial help from friends and family to help with getting started again, so strongly did I feel about stripping away obligations and indebtedness. At the time I knew no better, and at times later on, I sometimes felt that I had made my new start unnecessarily difficult by not accepting some of the generosity sent my way.

Today I believe that many women in the generation after me view women's roles differently. Most of the women I know in that generation are married to men who involve themselves with their houses and children. I hope that these young women consider their roles to be of equal value to that of their husbands, whether they work outside their homes or not. I hope they are clear about making their needs known, and fierce about having them met. I hope they hold them of equal value to the needs of every other member of the family.

Today other women sometimes tell me they envy me my passion for flying. "I wish I had something like that," Margie tells me. "I don't think I remember what my passions were."

On the other hand, Valerie, who paints primitives I find delicious, can hardly contain herself when she tells me how much she loves teaching art.

"I love it I love it I love it!" she cries.

My friend Ginny, who grew up in a wealthy New York family, was dreadfully unhappy at the first school to which she was sent. When at length she was withdrawn and placed in the progressive Lincoln School, she discovered herself, and was delighted.

"When I grow up," she told herself, "I'm going to make a school where kids can be safe and happy." When her own family had grown, her work as a psychological social worker reminded her how many children needed such a school, and she remembered her dream, and acted on it.

Today the Atrium School stands as one of the genuinely innovative and joyous primary schools in the Boston/Cambridge area.

But how can a woman go about discovering or rediscovering her passions? The time of her own dreams may feel like such a long time ago.

There are, I think, things she can do. She can note what books, movies, TV shows and videos make her truly excited and happy. She can think back to school days and recall what classes, school clubs, trips or activities interested her. In what courses was she inspired to excel? What were the things she repeatedly went out of her way to do?

When I was a child we sometimes played the game, "If you could be an animal, what animal would you be?" My answer was always the same, and I knew why. I would be a bird. They built nests and raised families, but they could fly.

A couple of miles from the house where I grew up, a grass field with a large oak at one end served as the local airport. If I saw a small plane fly over my house I would often toss a book into the basket of my bicycle and pedal the dirt roads through woods and fields. There, under the oak, I would lie reading, sometimes for hours, waiting to see if a plane would take off or land. Today this same area is black-topped, has proper runways and a small tower. The oak tree is gone, but not my memory of longing to rise above the earth, to be a part of the world over the world, where the view is the God's eye view that belongs to flight.

Again, pay attention to what you dream. Keep a dream journal, join a dream group, seek the help of a therapist who will help interpret those nightly visions. Like Jung, I believe that the inside knows what is happening in anyone's life before the outside does.

Think, listen, meditate. In quiet moments, free of the "stuff" of life, the essence of who you are and who you might like to become may surface, and rise to the front of consciousness.

Of course there have always been women who defied the strictures of their day, gender, or race to become who they felt they were born to be. Some women, such as Marie Curie, refused to accept the strictures of her time, and became a scientist.

Politically, Susan B. Anthony and Elizabeth Cady Stanton suffered almost unbearable ridicule and humiliation to work for women's rights.

In aviation, Bessie Coleman overcame rigid prejudice against both race and gender to become the first African-American woman to obtain a pilot's license, even if she had to go abroad at first to get it.

But these women were exceptions. In my life I settled into traditional women's roles, did the best job I could, and waited to feel fulfilled.

This is not to say that the job of raising a family isn't crucially important, extremely time consuming, constantly interruptive of anything else one may be trying to do, and just plain difficult. But it doesn't get you off the hook as far as being who you were meant to be. And it doesn't last forever.

In her book *Media's Folly*, Tanya Wilkenson maintains that while the general idea of caring for a home and family is revered in our culture, specific people and particular situations seldom are. If it is necessary for people to be valued for what they do in order to feel self-esteem, what does this mean to those who find themselves in this situation?

And when it's over, when the children are grown and on their own, what then? The average woman will have thirty or forty years to do with as she will.

Today I rarely attend cocktail parties, but when I do, I notice that topics of conversation seldom include the newest in scientific discoveries, ideas surfacing in education, or current political theory. Instead they appear to remain centered on the same things they were years ago, when I attended these parties more often. These include: where have you been and where are you going, and where have your children been and where are they going?

I remember such a party some years ago where I noticed a hard, narrow, blond woman, bearing the nickname of a small rodent, who had become distraught. She and her husband had just returned from a winter vacation in Florida. Someone had asked her if she'd attended the dog races, and when forced to admit she hadn't, had been told she "missed it." Dog racing, it seemed, was at that moment the thing to do.

"But honey," she wailed to her husband, "we missed it! We missed going to the dogs." It occurred to me that I wasn't altogether sure this was true. Many people I know who have reached retirement age cite travel as one of the goals to which they now aspire. Some of my friends immerse themselves in the language, art, history and culture of the area to which they will go, and afterwards, find their trip a time of general broadening, growth and joy. Others seem content with a litany of where they went, what they did and where they stayed, liberally interspersed with the adjective "marvelous."

Each of us, I believe, arrives on this planet with special gifts and talents. When we push against the barriers that keep us from bringing these to fruition, and take the chances we must take to make these happen, only then, it seems to me, can we come to know the deepest of life's joys. When we set aside the constraints of "being a lady," a "good girl," or of trying to be the person someone else wants us to be, only then do we, as Thoreau says of his experiment at Walden Pond, "advance confidently in the direction of our dreams, and live the life we've imagined." It's then that we "meet with success unexpected in common hours."

When I left my old life in the east and set out for a new one in the west, I had very little idea of what I would find. I knew I needed a job. I knew I wanted a life that was simple and real. I knew that family and friends would continue to be a vital part of my life, but I no longer felt driven to be the capstone in the arch of family. Now it was my turn. It was time to stop holding up the sky and get up into it.

CHAPTER THREE

"Who, me?" "Play the cello?" "Get a doctorate?" "Learn to fly?" "I'd love to, but…." "Build a plane?" "Who me?"

For eleven years I lived across the street from one of the best known teaching airports in the Northeast. I always attended the air shows there and loved them, but in all that time it never occurred to me, not once, not even for an instant, that I could learn to fly.

Of course there was a financial aspect to this, and I will address finances a bit later, but there were other reasons why I had no clue.

Many women, particularly in my generation, were taught in subtle ways through the culture, books, magazines, churches, TV, and movies, that their needs were not valid. They were encouraged instead, to look for fulfillment not in developing their own talents, but through the reflection of their families, and through acquisition.

"If you're not happy," the message said, "it's because you don't have stuff. You need a bigger house, another car, and don't forget, shopping is the answer to everything! And if you have stuff and you're still not happy, you need more stuff, different stuff."

This message to acquire is still all around us, and it is still utterly wrong. True joy has come to me only after taking on new challenges, and working hard to accomplish them. The more of our gifts we can put to good use the more satisfied we are.

I'm not speaking here about the genuine momentary pleasures of life, a new outfit, a good meal, a happy day with friends and family, but of something deeper. It doesn't mean there will never be a bad day, a close scrape or a real tragedy. It does mean that when someone is working to use as much of her-or himself as possible, attempting to reach and stretch and grow, a basic and profound joy underlies all that person does. It maintains and sustains that person, erupting to the surface when things go well, and providing a basic undercurrent of steadiness when they don't.

Part of this process means trying new things and taking chances. I once signed up for some Harvard extension courses for credit. A fellow classmate could not believe I had done this.

"How can you let someone else grade you?" she cried in horror. An excellent student all her life, this was never-the-less a chance she was unable to take. I did, and I'm happy to say those Harvard As have served me well. In addition, the repeated relocation of these classes seemed always to include a broken toilet. In sheer frustration I learned to fix various kinds of malfunctioning toilets, and this skill has also served me well, although this was not what I had expected to learn at Harvard.

When I speak of taking chances I'm not advocating foolhardiness. But most challenges require making oneself vulnerable in some way. Starting a different life, a new job, learning to play a musical instrument or to speak a different language all require putting yourself on the line, daring to become once more a beginner. It means taking the chance of failure. But without it there can be no real success.

Because women have often found themselves encouraged to derive their sense of themselves through others—husband, child, grandchild—this has not always been obvious to them. Of course these people can be extremely important parts of a woman's life. They certainly were and are for me. I cherish memories of the magic my father made of life, of the confidence he gave me, I revel in the people my children have become, and delight in my grandchildren. But none of this gets me off the hook. I can't live a life that's real if I live it only through the reflections of others.

A lot of people speak of marriage as a partnership, but I know of few in my generation that look like fifty-fifty propositions.

In his book *Yeager, An Autobiography*, Chuck Yeager tells of an exception to this. While he describes a career in aviation that began as a World War II fighter pilot and continued as the first person to break the sound barrier, his wife Glennis tells of the early years of their marriage. They produced four children quickly, and like most men of that era, Chuck was busy with work, often away from home on assignment, and little involved with raising his children. It was well ahead of the women's movement when Glennis wrote: "If you raise a man's children and run his household, you're an equal partner, and deserve to share equally in his income. I just decided half is half, and that's how it's going to be. I insisted on having my own savings account and property in my own name."

Not many women of her era were as clear-sighted as Glennis Yeager, but because she appreciated what she did, so did her husband. They continued their partnership not only after their children were grown, but also for many years until her death.

In or out of marriage, if we mean to be who we are, we will have to declare for that person. If a woman does not value what she does, if she accepts the judgment most people put on it, nobody else will value it either.

When I at last did decide to learn to fly, it did not come easily.

On a teacher's salary I needed and need to save for every lesson and for every time I fly. In addition, although my fine motor skills are good, because of a mixed dominance (I am right-handed and left-eyed dominate), my gross motor skills are not. With patience the brain can compensate, but it takes practice.

Then there is a third factor, subtle, pernicious, and so deeply ingrained as to be on nearly a cellular level.

"Who do you think you are?" "Why can't you be good?" "Nobody wants to hear what you have to say."

"Oh, so you know everything better than all the experts."

All the strictures that serve to turn a gender into second class citizens lurk just below the surface for many women who grew up when I did. It can cut off your legs every time you try to walk. Or to fly.

Amazingly, these voices often came and come from other women. It's always been a mystery to me why this should be so. The only guess I can give is that they act out of ignorance and fear.

I once went to a gathering where a large loaf cake was served as a part of the celebration. A friend whose demeanor had always suggested to me depression, cut the cake. As she handed out the pieces she proclaimed in a good strong voice, "I'll take the broken piece."

"See me?" she seemed to say. "See how sweet I am? How self-effacing? See how by accepting this role I proclaim my second-class status?"

It was fear, too, that I found at the bottom of what I felt when I told myself over and over, "I can do this. I can do this." Although I suspect that there is some trepidation for nearly everyone who learns to fly, for me it seemed even more difficult.

Sometimes I wonder how it happened that I went from not giving a thought to learning to fly to deciding to do it.

It took a long time, and it came bit by bit.

When I set out on my own for a new life in the Southwest, I did so because I felt I had no choice. I could no longer accept the life in which I found myself. If I were going to survive I would need to begin all over again, and to do it in a place where every vista on the New England highways, and every stop on the big city subways did not hold bittersweet memories.

So it was that I found myself in Santa Fe, New Mexico, early one summer, with no money and no job. I needed to find some work until school started in the fall and I could find a job teaching.

I had always liked to paint. Not pictures, but walls, tables, chairs. All kinds of things in my house had consistently changed color. So it happened that through a friend I met the owner of a small painting company who agreed to take me on as a journeyman painter for the summer. Each morning I set out to work carrying a lunch pail, and for the first time in my life no one asked me if I would "like" to do something, or if I thought I "could" do it. I was simply told to go up on the "big" ladder and paint the third floor dormer, and I did it. I was told to take the truck and clear out all the contents, including many heavy pieces, from the basement of a local government building, and I did it. I delivered material to the local state prison. I hung out of high windows painting nearly inaccessible spots. I even braved a haunted house, where I worked all day alone except for the ghost, whom I thought I felt moving along behind me wherever I went.

One morning I set out to oil the deck of a house near a site where the rest of the crew was working. It was hot, and before I had finished I had run out of the water I had brought with me, and I knocked on the door to ask for a drink.

The woman who answered the door looked me up and down and told me to use the hose.

The following week a friend treated me to a glorious production at the Santa Fe Opera. During the intermission she took me to the VIP pavilion. There, whom should I spot but the woman whose deck I had oiled only the week before. I was astonished when she came over to us, and fawningly introduced herself to my friend. Then she turned to me.

"And don't I know you?" she cooed.

"Yes," I told her, "you do. Last week when I knocked on your door you refused me a drink of water."

By the time that summer had turned to fall and I had found a teaching job, I discovered that I had acquired a lot more self confidence than I had felt at the season's start. The physical challenges I'd accepted had, I found, translated well into other areas of my life. By the time I was back in the classroom I moved with a lot more assurance than I'd ever felt before.

From my first days in Santa Fe I'd heard tales of a one-room schoolhouse some twenty-five miles south of the city. Built twenty years earlier by "hippie" parents, the passive-solar structure housed children, three to nine. Invited to visit, I became intrigued by the mix of children, the open philosophy, and the obvious joy the students seemed to find in teaching what they had just learned to the next children down in line.

When, a couple of years later, I learned that the teacher at The Children's Workshop wanted to move on, I eagerly took on the project. Thus began seven of the most exhilarating and joyous years of the more than thirty I have spent in the classroom.

We boasted a computer and an outhouse, and during the winter I arrived early to chop wood for the stove that took the chill off before the effective solar heat of the building warmed the large room. During the first year I was there we had no running water, and I carried all the water we used from home. With anywhere from eight to fifteen children enrolled, I was able, with the aid of an assistant when there were more than ten children, to see that each child worked in an individualized curriculum in reading and math. Science and social studies we all did together, and lessons included visitations to a site the children called "the owl place," and from where they collected owl pellets which they brought back to the classroom and eagerly dissected to see what the raptor had eaten.

We built a blind from which we watched a golden eagle and her three fledglings. We voted on where we would venture each day, and thus learned about basic democracy. Children began reading at whatever age they proved ready, and it was nearly always an older child who took a younger through the beginning reader for the first time. When this happened, their joy and mine flew in all directions like fireworks.

Because the parents were involved with the school, bringing and collecting children, helping in the classroom, and appearing on communal workdays to attend to building and ground maintenance, and sharing a "pot luck" meal, I came to know most of them well. Many had cleared their land and built their houses with their own hands, much as their predecessors had done a hundred and fifty years before. I felt I had come to know and respect genuine pioneers, and in the process had become a bit of one myself.

Eventually a new public school in the neighborhood saw the demise of the little school, but by that time I knew not only that I had enjoyed the teaching experience of a lifetime, but also that now I could draw from inside myself strengths and abilities I could use for the rest of my life.

CHAPTER FOUR

Cailyn, one of the children who attended the rural one-room schoolhouse where I taught for seven years, was about six when she came bouncing into school one morning.

"Hey guess what?" she called to us all. "My family's very rich!"

I thought of Cailyn's young family, scraping together everything they could to erect a hand-built homestead on a beautiful piece of land some four bone-shaking miles off New Mexico route fourteen. Cailyn and her younger brother arrived at school each morning in a car whose original color was long past distinguishing, and whose hood and door were tied into place with bits of rope. When the engine was extinguished, several loud backfires would be emitted, causing the children to call it "the popcorn car."

"That's great, Cailyn," I told her.

"Yeah," she continued, "We love each other very much. We got a beautiful new baby, my Daddy's building us a wonderful house, and everywhere we look we see mountains. And," she reiterated, "we love each other very much. We just don't have any money."

Some time later I was hiking with a friend. Pat was bemoaning the fact that she detested being "dirt poor." Her nondescript car, she told me, was mostly unpaid for, her credit cards were maxed out, and she hated her life. I thought of Pat's shabby apartment with its worn couch and rickety tables. The attractive corner fireplace had been closed up to prevent heat escaping up the chimney, and a broken chair had been dragged in front of it. She knew, Pat confided, that all her troubles would be over if only she made a decent salary, or if, that cure-all for everything, she "had money."

I felt some little guilt listening to her, as I had just purchased a small townhouse which, although I couldn't afford to live in it, provided me a bit of investment for the future. In addition I had no debts, and whenever I could save for one, I was taking a flying lesson. It came as a real shock, therefore, when in disgust, Pat confided to me the amount of her salary. Her yearly income it transpired, was exactly twice mine.

Many of the terms we use in flying are excellent metaphors for life. One of my favorites, the manner by which one controls stability, speed, ascent and descent, and safety in the air, is the plane's attitude.

In his autobiographical books, most of which were written during his eighth decade, the comedian George Burns discussed life's difficulties. Some of the things that happened to people, he felt, were just the luck of the draw, beyond anyone's ability to change. The one thing over which they did have control, he thought, was their attitude. He thought that made all the difference.

Managing the funds one does have can be a big help. Keeping track of where funds go is important if this is something that is poorly understood. More than once I have heard people say, "I just don't know where the money went!"

Pat was one of those who repeatedly told me that she had absolutely no idea where her money had gone. To know is essential if you want to plan ahead, and planning ahead financially is important. People who successfully manage their funds have many ways to do this. Surely large sums can require the help of a professional money manager. But many of us who do not have large funds, have other ways to deal with this.

What I do is to keep separate checking or savings accounts for everything requiring large sum expenditures: taxes, insurance, car repair, etc., and of course I have one just for the plane. I put some part of each paycheck into each account, and then when, for example, car insurance comes due, it's not necessary to scramble to pay the bill. The funds are there. Other people have other ways to manage, and to them my way may sound foolish, but it works for me.

Some people keep careful records of every single expenditure, even small ones, and this may be a good idea for awhile if one is unsure what happens to monies. Some make a budget.

For the first years I was on my own I planned each month's expenditures carefully. Now, when I allot funds to each account, this takes care of itself. I can tell how much is available at any time, and can plan accordingly.

Now, this does not mean that things always come out even. There are times when a certain amount of juggling is necessary, but I keep track, and adjust when I'm able.

The other thing that is important if one wants to achieve goals, is to set priorities. If you wish to save for a lifelong dream, such as buying a sailboat or a house, you'd best not sign up for a balloon safari in Africa, or a little ride on the QE II. This may sound self-evident, but I am constantly astonished at how many people I know go into debt to take an expensive trip or make a huge purchase. It's an individual choice, of course, but if you have a dream you want to come true, then you have to set aside funds when you plan, and keep that money sacred.

Credit cards are marvelous, I think. They allow me to buy that extra gift, meal or tee shirt covered with pictures of biplanes, that doesn't fit into the budget at the moment. They allow ordering purchases by phone, so that an airline ticket with an especially low price, or some sale item, can be nailed into place on the spot. But I never buy anything with a credit card that I can not pay off totally when the next bill arrives, either from the next month's budget or from a special fund where I've saved for these items. I simply do not feel that I can afford to pay fifteen or twenty percent more for things than they cost. Credit card interest is not in my budget.

People often ask me how much it costs to learn to fly. My answer is always the same. It costs the price of the next lesson. Again, this is the "small steps" idea.

There is no doubt that had unlimited funds been available, I would have been able to learn to fly a lot sooner. So what? Was this something I wanted enough to save for a lesson, take extra jobs when I could get them, forego other purchases or activities that would have given me pleasure, in order to get what I wanted? I was willing to be single-minded to get what I wanted. Do whatever you need to do, short of robbing a bank, to get what you want.

Somewhere along the way in the process of learning to fly it occurred to me that I was going to a lot of trouble, and spending a lot of money to learn to fly, and that when I finished I would have nothing to fly. I just didn't see how I could squeeze the price of an airplane, or even a share in one, out of a kindergarten teacher's salary. Then I remembered Thoreau and his hut on Walden Pond. When the first winter on the pond approached, he knew he needed a fireplace and chimney. So, he would do as he had done before, he would build them. But he didn't know how. "So it was clear," he wrote, "that I needed to go to the library and get a book." So it was clear to me that I could do the same. I could get a book and some plans, and I could build an airplane.

When I announced my intention to my eldest son, he—like my other children—was supportive.

"Only thing is, Ted," I told him, "I don't know how to build an airplane."

"Don't worry, Mum," he said. "Just learn how to build wing ribs. Send me the plans and I'll build the forms. When you get those finished, learn how to build the next thing. Keep doing that, and pretty soon you'll have an airplane." Already I belonged to the Experimental Aircraft Association. Surely I could call on these people, many of whom had built planes, for advice.

But tools and materials? I would need special woods, for example, and tools. At that time, I owned no power tools. But Ted had said he'd make "jigs" for the wing ribs, and I had hand tools. I sent for forty dollars' worth of the required kind of wood, known as "capstripping," and set to work.

I thought of Joseph Campbell's quote about determining where you were going. "When you are on your path," he'd said, "invisible hands reach out to help you."

The rest would have to take care of itself.

One evening while I was working, my friend Constanze came through the door. She held a ragged bit of paper in her hand. She'd torn it from the back of the *Utne Reader*, she told me.

"I have no idea if you have any interest in this," she told me, "but you never know, so I thought I'd show it to you."

The scrap of paper told of an organization with the rather surprising title of The Thanks Be To Grandmother Winifred Foundation that gave grants to women past a certain age who were engaged in enterprises that could be of help to other women. Since I planned to write about my project as a grandmother building an airplane to encourage other women to do their dreams regardless of their age, I decided to send for information.

When the specifics for application arrived, I was startled to discover that the deadline for application was less than a week away.

"Well," I told Constanze, " I don't think anybody's going to give me a grant for materials to build an airplane, but I need to signal the universe that I've got a project going. I really don't want to stay up the next couple of nights to write this grant, but part of making a dream come true is doing the homework."

So I stayed up and I wrote the grant.

About this same time I happened to speak on the phone with my godmother, Alice. Since I was child she had seemed like a fairy godmother, always choosing the perfect gift. When I became a teenager, the dream dress would always arrive before the "big event," though she had no way of knowing when these were due. They always fit perfectly, and when I went on to college, she and her husband often would arrive to take me away from college food for a good meal. When I became a new mother, the perfect piece of baby equipment arrived by mail.

When I told Alice that I was learning to fly there was a long pause. "How old are you?" she asked at last.

When I told her, and added that I was starting to build a plane, there was a really long pause.

"Well," she said at last, "I guess you can do anything you want to do." When Alice left the planet at ninety-five, I was crushed. She was the last one left from the preceding generation, she had always had a special respect for who I was, and I had adored her.

So I ought not to have been surprised to find that in her will she had left me a thousand dollars for my airplane.

The notice that arrived in the mail to tell me to pick up a registered letter at the post office felt like an annoyance, until I opened it and to astonishment of other post office patrons, let out a whoop. The Thanks Be To Grandmother Winifred Foundation had granted me the monies for the wood for the plane! When it arrived from Canada, my second son, Art, kindly met it in Albuquerque where he had moved, having also fallen in love with the Southwest. He saw it through customs, and for some months the long, cylindrical tube hung from the ceiling in my office and out over the dining room table.

If you have a mother who is building an airplane, you don't have to think too hard about what to get her for Christmas. In due course, a belt sander, orbital sander, drill, and various hand tools arrived with the Yuletide. By the time the wing ribs, all sixty-eight of which had been crafted totally by hand, were finished, I was able to begin on the "tail feathers." I was no longer using exclusively hand tools.

As it happened, the woman who had begun the grant from which the funds for the wood had come, had continued to provide moral support. She had lent me two delightful, privately published books written by an uncle, chronicling two flights, one in Africa and one around the world, that he had undertaken in the late twenties and early thirties. She had sent me a book about early women pilots, and often provided newspaper articles about women who flew. I was part way through reading one of these about Amelia Earhart, when a check for a thousand dollars fell out.

So I worked and I thought. Advice from EAA members, especially the technical consultant Jeff Scott, (and later Will Fox), helped, but while I worked I wondered in some concern about an engine. This would surely be the biggest expense, and as yet I had no idea how I would finance this.

Each fall the school where I taught, now that the one-room schoolhouse had closed, held a fund-raising bazaar. It was fun. All day the children ran up to me to share the small prizes they had won at the game booths, and parents and other teachers stopped to chat. Late in the afternoon a barrel was rolled onto the stage and the raffle took place.

This particular year I had bought a ticket, telling the universe I needed an engine. Mark, one of the parents, turned the handle of the barrel to mix the tickets, and chose a child to reach in for a ticket which he read to himself. "Wow!" he cried. "This is going to make this person very happy!" Then he read the number: 380.

"Well," I thought, "that's a mistake. 380 is my number."

It was no mistake. I had won ten thousand dollars. I would have my engine.

While I worked and learned, the "invisible hands" Joseph Campbell had told about had reached out to help me. And, as I was to discover, they were not through yet. Not by a long shot.

When people say to me, "Oh I'd love to be able to do such and such, but I just can't afford it," I understand that this is simply not true. Either they have not yet thought through and discovered the way, or are not willing to save and wait, or they simply don't want it enough.

On one of his self-help tapes, Indian-American Dr. Depak Chopra tells the story of a certain guru, who, when explaining a worthwhile project he was planning to some followers, was asked from where the money to fund the project would come.

"'Twill come," the guru replied, "from wherever it is at the moment."

If you manage whatever funds you have well by finding methods that work for you, hold to your priorities, practice patience and are willing to take one small step at a time, you can make nearly anything happen. Try not to worry too much if things take longer than you think they are "supposed" to take. The ideas our culture puts forward about money and possessions border on the ridiculous. Nobody needs to buy into them. It is possible to stay focused. It is after all your attitude that will put your plane into the air.

CHAPTER FIVE

I live in a house that is somewhere between three and four hundred years old. The basic structure was some sort of outbuilding for one of the original ranches built on land granted the inhabitants of this area by the king of Spain in the fifteen hundreds. Their descendents still live on the same land. Every spring they, and all the rest of us who live along Acequia Madre (Mother Ditch), meet on a given day and clean out the ditch. This has been happening for four hundred years.

The main room of my house measures about nine by twelve, and there is a small office almost eight by eleven. The house is constructed of huge, ancient adobe blocks. It has a tiny dining area, a galley kitchen, and abnormally low ceilings. There is a bathroom and one rather small closet. The perfect place to build an airplane!

Or at least to start to build an airplane.

Spring had passed. I knew because the wands of Castilian rose bushes that come up each spring between the inside wall and floor in my house had dried into stiff tails. I've spent the summer building the horizontal and vertical stabilizers, the rudder and fin, on a level "table" on the floor of my office while the two snakes peer inquisitively from their tank and the cats come in to look and flatten their ears. Now these parts hang from the vigas (indoor crossbeams), and at night I lie in bed and watch them move gently in the breeze from the window fan as though eager to fly. As it turns out, they never will.

One hot summer day I arrive home to find a message on my answer phone to call the office at school. I'm given the name and phone number of someone who would like to come see my project. I am dispirited, having done about as much work on my plane as I can in my tiny house, and wait several days to call.

When I do, Tom Hill comes to visit, and several days later phones to ask if I would like to use his garage as a place to continue building, and I take him up on the offer. Eventually Tom, who has been building remote control models for twenty years, admits to a desire to work full scale.

Four months later, after I've sold my townhouse, we buy a warehouse together, and for a total of two and a half years work steadily together. Tom, with his great model experience, leads the way, and I will be grateful for his invaluable help forever.

During this time I've learned to use a router and all manner of power tools, a lot about reading blue prints, and quite a bit more about how planes fly.

One evening during the time we are working together, our friend Doug Ried appears. He has a thick book with many aeronautical tables, and tells us sadly that according to the tables, we have much too much wing area for our tail. It just will not work. We confer, and determine to redesign and rebuild the tail. We do, and this goes amazingly quickly, and it seems huge. Tom's help is especially valued now, but I am also surprised at how much my own building skills have improved.

After nearly two and a half years of working together, Tom is eager to build a plane of his own, and I make plans to move up to the EAA hanger in Los Alamos. I will have my own space now, my own workshop and tools, and I'll be in a real hangar.

For several years people from the EAA have been working on rebuilding a hangar that had belonged to our dear friend Harley Lane, who had passed on. They had redesigned and rebuilt the whole infrastructure, and put in a cement floor. I'd helped when and where I could, and now was granted a quarter of the hanger where I might work.

It's taken a while to get to this place.

Back when I'd first thought of building a plane, I'd debated what kind.

I knew I wanted to work with wood and cloth, not metal and rivets. Whenever I'd gone to a fly-in and walked the flight line where the planes were parked, it was always the biplanes that drew me like a magnet.

The Nuport, SE5, the Spad reproductions, the gloriously huge Steermans, the gleaming Wacos and Hatzes, these enchanted me. I can remember standing in front of a genuine antique Gypsy Moth whose wings actually folded, and finally understanding what a friend meant when he spoke of "lusting after a plane." I wanted to jump up and down and scream, "I want this plane!"

It would have been easiest to choose a kit, but most of these produced planes that were five-eights or seven-eights the size of the originals, and to me, even the seven-eights size never looked quite right.

Bernie Pietenpol's plans for his monoplane first appeared in Popular Mechanics in the late twenties or early thirties, and people have been building the Sky Camper ever since. Sometime during the sixties, Chad Willie and his dad had added a second wing and produced something that looked more like an old "Jenny," the World War I surplus biplane that most "barnstormers" had used during what is often called "the golden era of flight," than it looked like the original Pietenpol. With a twenty-nine-and-a-half wing span it was full-sized, and looked to me "right." An open cockpit, tandem-seated biplane made of wood and cloth meant to me the origins and essence of flying. I wanted not so much to fly my plane cross-country, but rather to fly for fun over the local countryside. I wanted the opportunity to do real "bugs in the teeth" flying, and to have it near at hand. I wanted to be able to fly my grandchildren around in a plane I had helped to build myself.

My grandchildren. When they were born I gave serious thought to what I could pass along to them that might be meaningful. Since I do not live near them I would not be able to see then as often as I would like, or be a part of their everyday life. Nor would I, as a teacher, be able to secure their financial futures.

What I decided I might be able to communicate to them was that life was about following passions. If I showed them my passion for something, they might see this, and eventually know the joy of discovering and following their own passions. If I could do this, I would indeed be able to give them a valuable gift. (At this writing, all three want to become pilots.)

Does anyone need to know how to do something before taking it on? Not if he/she is not afraid of learning and doing new things, of working hard, and is not embarrassed to ask for help when it's needed.

From the start of my project I've counted on the guidance and support of many of the EAA members, and have always been grateful for these. Their kindness and help has always been appreciated, and their hours of airplane talk and stories a joy.

As I started to build, it wasn't long before I discovered that the cap-strips,(the top piece of the wing ribs), needed to be pre-bent. The curve of the top piece of each rib was such that, if the first ten or twelve inches of the piece were not softened and bent beforehand, it would break when pressed into the form. Here I went off on my own. The suggestions I received from EAA members were mathematically disturbing or physically puzzling, so I came up with my own idea.

I took my oversized pasta pot, and using three or four strips at a time, boiled the first foot or so for about an hour. This insured that they were well softened, permeated as they were with moisture. Then, after removing several days worth of underwear from it the top dresser drawer, I closed firmly the dry end of the strips drawer. The other end I slipped through a loop of strong nylon yarn which had been fastened to a screw eye in an overhead viga (you will remember that this is an adobe style exposed beam). At the softened end I hung a brick, and in a matter of days I had three or four capstrips that fit perfectly into their jig, or form, without breaking. The national Pietenpol newsletter told its readers that Arlene Walsh was "cookin' ribs!"

From there it was only a matter of a drop cloth on my living room floor, an old movie on the TV, and I was ready to construct a wing rib. So I did. I made sixty-eight of them, all by hand. Then I sanded them.

When the fuselage kit had arrived from Calgary, Canada (top quality Sitka spruce having become impossible to purchase in this country in lengths long enough for my needs), my son Art, who had seen it through customs and stored it in a local cellar, helped me fasten it to the ceiling in the little "office" room of my house.

From there it progressed to Tom Hill's garage, and then on to the warehouse. Then I was working in a real hangar. From having had no power tools, I had moved to a workbench and shelves full of them, all organized and carefully labeled.

Several years before, at a fly-in in Arizona, I had spoken to three older men, who together flew their World War I replica biplanes in an act they billed as "The Dawn Patrol." I had noticed that all three planes used Lycoming engines, and individually, I asked each pilot why. All three gave me essentially the same answer; all three thought that for this type of plane, it was the best. From then on, Lycoming was at the top of my list for an engine.

One winter evening while I was working with Tom, he suggested that I was not doing my "homework" looking for an engine. He thought I needed to go to the local airports and talk to the mechanics, telling them what I wanted.

"You just think an engine's going to fall from the sky," he laughed. I knew though, that the two people most tuned in to what was available had been alerted, and felt that one or the other would find me an engine, and Jeff

Scott did. One of Jeff's old school chums had an uncle who was ill, and selling off the lifetime collection of flying paraphernalia in his hangar.

Jeff and Doug Ried drove down to southern New Mexico where the hangar was located, and Doug bought a hand-made Taylorcraft plane, and Jeff an assortment of airplane equipment and tools. He had carefully read the log of an engine that was for sale, and he called me at once.

It'll last longer than you will," he told me, and I grabbed at the opportunity. There was nobody I trusted more in these matters than Jeff. So it was that on Easter Sunday morning that year, as we unloaded the Lycoming 0290 engine from the back of Doug's truck, I looked over at Tom, and it was my turn to laugh.

"I just think an engine's going to fall from the sky," I said.

Pietenpol Aerial Biplane designed by Chad Wille. Photo courtesy of Chad Wille.

CHAPTER SIX

It is time to speak of Henry David.

We all have our guiding spirits, our mentors, the giants upon whose shoulders we stand when we reach for the stars.

The summer I was thirteen my father took my best friend Margi and me from our homes in Connecticut to Concord, Massachusetts, to visit the family home of Louisa May Alcott. Orchard House had been used as a model for the last two film versions of *Little Women*, and was open to the public. The story was a favorite of both Margi and myself, and we soaked up everything we could find about the Alcotts and where they had lived. We had a marvelous time, and I still have snapshots of each of us jumping the fence in front of the house, just like Jo. As we drove out of Concord heading toward home, just outside the village, we passed the bluest body of water I had ever seen.

"Look, look!" I cried as we passed, "look at that blue pond!"

Most of our New England ponds, including the one in which I regularly swam, were light brownish in color, but Walden Pond in 1949 was still unpolluted, and a clear blue. Later I would discover that Thoreau had written that he could always tell ice cut from Walden when he saw it for sale in the streets of Boston, by its color. The next time I would see the pond, in 1954, although a local battle against a nearby trailer park that had tried to build near it had been won, it was not before the water had been polluted, and the blue color gone forever.

"That's Walden Pond," my father told me. "Do you know about Henry Thoreau?"

I didn't, but the following day my dad gave me a copy of *Walden*, and I retired to the attic with it and a basket of apples, and there, while the dust motes danced in the light from the dusky window, I ate apples and fell in love.

There are not many passions begun at thirteen that last into adulthood, but my "affair" with Henry David has.

Always adults had cautioned me, a dreamy child, against "building castles in the air." But Thoreau congratulated me for doing this, and told me, "Now go put foundations under them."

He told me that he had gone out from the village of Concord to live at Walden Pond, and he told me why. "I went to the woods because I wished to live deliberately, to front only the essential facts of life, and see what it had to teach, and not, when I came to die, discover that I had not lived."

Like most children of my era, I was often admonished to behave, to be "a good girl." Imagine my delight to hear: "The greatest part of what my neighbors call good I believe in my soul to be bad, and if I repent of anything, it is very likely my good behavior. What demon possessed me that I behaved so well?"

This was pretty heady stuff for a thirteen-year-old, fresh from Louisa May Alcott.

In the course of time I discovered that Thoreau had admonished his readers against American materialism in the first half of the nineteenth century. I wonder what he would think of it today.

Sometimes people have expressed to me the thought that Thoreau took the path he did because as a "nere-do-well" he could do nothing else.

In fact, Thoreau's family owned a small pencil factory, and during the short time he worked there, Henry invented the graphite formula used in pencils to this day. Every time you pick up a pencil you make a direct connection with the tenant of Walden Pond. Thoreau sold the enterprise when, as he said, "It threatened to make me rich."

The "essential fact's of life" that Thoreau wanted to confront, contemplate and write about were more important to him than wealth and what it could buy. He preferred to: "be seated on a pumpkin and have it all to myself, than be crowded on a velvet cushion." He found it difficult to: "stand on the meetings of two eternities, the past and the future which is precisely the present moment, weighted with gold or silver fetters."

From Thoreau I learned that it was OK not to follow the crowd, but could "march to a different drummer." With the years I have come to see how these ideas could deepen one's sense of integrity, as well as the sense of what's real.

Another thing I learned from Thoreau was that we do not always understand the ultimate ramifications of what we do.

After its publication, *Walden* was scarcely a best seller. Obliged to buy most of the unsold copies to keep them from destruction, Henry dragged the boxes to an upstairs room in his mother's house and joked that he now owned a library of several hundred volumes, most of which he had written himself.

A lack of "accumulated dross" allowed Thoreau to stand for what he believed. When Emerson visited him as he spent a night in the Concord jail for refusing to pay taxes to a government that permitted slavery, Emerson queried, "Henry, what are you doing in there?" Peering through the bars Henry replied, "Waldo, what are you doing out there?"

Thoreau wrote of this experience in *Civil Disobedience* and went on with his life. He did what he thought was right and continued down his own particular road. He couldn't know that the concentric circles set in motion when he tossed his stone into Walden Pond would grow to include the world. He would never know that *Civil Disobedience* would influence the British

Labor movement, or that the slim volume of *Walden* was the one Gandhi kept beside his bed. The seeds of Indian independence were watered from Walden Pond.

When Franklin Delano Roosevelt took on the presidency of a nation terrified by the numbing influence of a crippling depression, he told that nation that "the only thing we have to fear is fear itself," and he quoted Thoreau.

When Thoreau wrote that obedience to unjust laws was immoral, he helped to set in motion a civil rights movement in his own country more than a hundred years after his death.

Henry Thoreau lived more than half a century before the invention of the airplane, but he helped me learn to fly.

The gentle ghosts who lead us from eternity inspire, lead, and guide. But not all our mentors need to be dead. I could never have done what I did and am doing without the support of family, friends and mentors.

My family remained enthusiastic throughout this process. If they thought, "What nutty thing is our mother up to now?" they never said it to me. Time and again I arrived home to find an encouraging message from a friend on my answering machine.

As I took my small steps forward, congratulatory gifts often arrived at my door. And nobody ever said to me, "What, are you still working on that?" Paul Dwyer, my first long-suffering flight instructor, must have many times wanted to suggest that I take up fishing. Instead, whenever I asked him if he really thought I could learn his reply was always the same. "I wouldn't take your money if I didn't think you could do it."

Learning to fly and building a plane, learning new things and taking new chances moved me into a different world. I came into my own in a way that helped me to become more authentic than ever before. What I found when this happened continues to amaze me. Others appeared to respond positively to someone who makes the effort to become the person they really are. Something in authenticity attracts. It holds within it the tremendous force that is the power of truth.

"Individuation" is the term psychologist Carl Jung used to describe the development of the unique self. It's a movement toward wholeness, toward becoming oneself, to achieving one's own potential.

What Jung called the "animus," the male part of the human psyche, in women it is often part of the unconscious; and this part that connects us to our creativity and takes us out into the world, can easily be projected onto a man. Too often in the era in which I came of age, this was subtly and not so subtly, encouraged. To dissolve my own real self into family relationships, I was told, would yield total satisfaction. It didn't, and my own authenticity was drained. So it was that I came to believe it was unladylike to "blow my own horn." I had been taught to proclaim my own niceness, my own self-effacingness, to "take the broken piece."

It came with some difficulty, therefore, for me to believe that my ultimate supporter must be myself. Words follow thoughts and actions follow words. That's how we create our lives, and in creating our lives, we create ourselves.

If you don't like your life, you are the only one who can change it, and you are the only one who has the power to do it. You can't do it alone; you will most likely need your supporters and mentors. But you can do it.

When the day came on which at last I soloed, I opened the door to the sky and walked through. When I wondered what I would see in this new realm, I was surprised to see someone walking toward me. It took a minute to understand that what showed at the end of this long corridor was a mirror, and that the person walking toward me was me.

CHAPTER SEVEN

Not long ago I happened upon a news program on TV that was featuring at that moment a bicycle club. Somewhere between fifteen and twenty people cycled past the camera, a few sitting upright like Agatha Cristie's Miss Marple riding into town, most assuming the correct aerodynamic position, bent over, riding quickly, and sporting helmets. Nobody seemed to be racing, but they rode steadily, intent, competent. Then I heard the voice-over. "This is the Centenarian Bicycle Club. To be a member, you have to be at least one hundred years old."

Being one hundred, it would seem, is not what it used to be. But then neither is fifty, sixty, seventy or eighty.

Health and fitness awareness, modern medical advances, and a burgeoning population (there are now twice as many people in the United States than there were when I was a child), means that more of us are going to live longer. To a great extent what we do with that time is up to us.

Recently a friend who had just turned sixty remarked to me that he supposed he had another ten years left in which to fly. I turned to him in consternation. "If you imagine that you'll only have ten more years left to fly, then that's what you'll have," I said. "Why don't you imagine instead that you'll fly till you're ninety-five, then if something comes up between now and then, deal with it." He was startled, but as he thought about it, said, "You know, you're right." Last I heard, he had a newer, faster plane, and was still flying.

As I write this I am watching a dance festival at Duke University. Four tap dancers are performing with tremendous energy. The announcer tells me they execute two shows a day, and all but one are in their early eighties, and the other is eighty-six. One performer says he has never enjoyed himself more, and never had better audiences. I can remember a time when dancers often considered themselves "past it" when they were thirty-five.

With the acceptance by a large part of the population as to what diet, exercise and new medications beneficial to longevity can mean, has come a healthier life style for many of us, young, and not so young. As we learn more it makes more sense to use that knowledge.

At the time that my father died of hypertension at forty-eight, not only did medications to control this not exist, but also no one seemed to know to tell him about diet and exercise, the possible help of meditation, or the fact that perhaps his pack-a-day cigarette habit wasn't doing him any good either. If I know better, then I have the option of doing better.

Some recent brain research results provide data that provide significant and astonishing implications concerning some kinds of dementia.

One study involved a group of nuns living somewhere in the northern part of the Midwestern United States. These women had been teachers, and as such had received more education than many women had in the early part of the twentieth century. This was one factor that figured in the results researchers saw much later.

Another important factor distinguished these women from others in similar organizations in their time and place. At the time they joined their order of nuns, they were required to agree that at certain specified intervals, every few years, they would take on a new intellectual challenge. They agreed to follow this endeavor through to completion, or to a certain degree of proficiency. They must learn a new language, to play a musical instrument, or do something commensurate, and they must repeat this at regular intervals.

As it happened, many of these women lived on to very advanced age, into their ninth or even tenth decade, and when they did die, often left their bodies to science. When their brains were autopsied, something astonishing appeared.

Although some of the brains did show signs of the lesions of Altzheimer's disease and of other forms of dementia, brain synapses had grown around these lesions, and the women while alive had evidenced no signs of dementia.

Although it was previously thought that creating new brain cells was impossible, that everyone was born with an immutable number of brain cells, this has recently been proved untrue. New brain cells can be created with new learning, and every time a new thing is learned, new brain synapses, the points of contact between neurons where nerve impulses are transmitted from one to another, are created.

Similarly, rats raised in void and sterile environments show far fewer brain synapses than rats raised in stimulating environments.

We know that other parts of the body are strengthened by use; muscles become stronger with use, (including the heart muscle), bones can increase their density with weight-bearing exercise, lung capacity can increase with exercise. It seems to make sense that learning in youth and young adulthood, followed by continuing intellectual challenges throughout life, may well postpone or even circumvent some types of age-related dementia.

Certainly it's true that many of us know elderly people who have continued to accept physical and mental challenges, and who as a result, continue to remain active and alert. Conversely, it's true that most of us are able to name some older people who appear to have "shut down," removed themselves from the mainstream, and, turning inward, seemed to fade. These people tend to repeat themselves endlessly, to expect others to show an overconcern with their own or others, health, and they may complain continually. They are seldom much fun to have around.

My friend Ruth Feldman first fell in love with the language and culture of Italy when she was a girl, in 1936. It was not, however, until she was fifty-five and her husband died suddenly, leaving her feeling at loose ends, that she began to take seriously her gift for languages. No longer, as she told me, able to see herself reflected in her husband, she began to create herself anew. Learning Italian and beginning to write poetry, she eventually produced several books of poetry in English and many more translations of Italian poetry. When she died at ninety-five, she left fifteen books, including a prize-winning translation of Primo Levy.

Recently a friend bemoaned to me all the things she had never got to do in her life. She had not earned an advanced university degree, spent time in India, taken the voice lessons she had so much wanted.

"But," she told me, "I never got the chance."

When she told me this she was thirty-five years old.

On the other hand, a couple of summers ago my dear friend Nancy Cobb performed Bach's Brandenburg Concerto Number Four on the recorder for over two hundred people. It was the first time she had performed for an audience that size, and she had had only two weeks to practice. She transposed from the key of G to the key of F, working especially hard, and the concert went very well. At the time, Nancy was eighty-one.

Today I identify with the insect Thoreau describes on the last page of Walden. He speaks of:

> ...a strong and beautiful bug which came out of the dry leaf of an old table of apple-tree wood, which had stood in a farmer's kitchen for sixty years, first in Connecticut, and afterwards in Massachusetts—from an egg deposited in the living tree many years earlier still, as appeared by counting the annual layers beyond it; which was heard gnawing out.... Who knows what beautiful and winged life, whose egg has been buried for ages under many concentric layers of woodenness in the dead dry life of society...may unexpectedly come forth...to enjoy its perfect summer life at last!

CHAPTER EIGHT

What is it to be who we really are?

Jessie Bean moved to Boston sometime during the late nineteen-fifties or early nineteen-sixties. Tall, lithe, cheerful, and with a slight air of mystery about her, she gained immediate popularity, especially among the city's eligible young men. In the course of time she settled upon an expatriate Englishman named Benjamin, and the two moved to the fashionable north shore where they settled, and eventually produced two fanciful and beguiling children. Popular and sought after, they socialized regularly, and although Jessie's humor and cheerfulness were much appreciated, her mysteriousness remained. Although upbeat and amusing, she remained an enigma. Again and again I heard the same comment, "But who IS Jessie Bean?"

Although an amalgam of attractive personality traits, for reasons unknown, the real Jessie Bean remained hidden and unavailable.

Feelings of inferiority may keep people from living lives that are real. Peggy was simply unable to tell the truth. She might have a perfectly good reason why she was unable to agree to some request, but again and again I heard her make up another, often foolish-sounding excuse. Anything that was hers, she was convinced, could not possibly be good enough.

During a course of study for an MBA at Duke University, my niece Kim fell in love with South America. Upon completion of her degree she accepted a job that paid less than others she was offered, because performing it enables her to travel and engage in business in countries she has come to love, and to interact with cultures about which she is able to learn more. This is who she is.

Who we really are is closely related to our passions. There may be times in all our lives when we must make decisions based on survival. In time these usually pass, and ideally we will be able to engage in doing the things we love and still make a living. When I sat in the middle of a kindergarten class, bantering with children whom I had some small hand in allowing to become as eager and open to learning as they were, I knew I was where I was supposed to be.

When you move, take a new job, accept a new friend, join a new organization, is this who you really are?

The courage to make the changes needed to become who we really are can be very great indeed. Big sacrifices can be involved, or the pain of working through blockages from past trauma. Often the way does not seem clear, and small steps are necessary, feeling our way as we go.

Issues from the past that are not cleared up can keep anyone from becoming who he/she really is. If these traumas are not worked through, the energy required to repress what has not been cleared can be terrific. In her memoir of her time spent with novelist John Gardner called *On Broken Glass*, Susan Thornton tells of the difficulty Gardner had holding down the guilt he felt for the death of a younger brother in an accident that had occurred when he was child. Because it was never totally cleared, it created a lifestyle that eventually resulted in Gardner's death.

Food, alcohol, drugs, shopping, can all be used to try to keep what has not been well dealt with from surfacing. Inability to trust others, and lack of the self-esteem needed to become real can also be a part of this.

The single welfare mother who became a PhD in psychiatry says she didn't accomplish this all at once. Swamped by the chores babies and a house created, she nevertheless decided to take two college courses and stick with them no matter what. When these felt right and she did well, she signed up for two more. So it went.

Karen Johnson, another welfare mom who created herself, did it through the small, grueling steps of comedy workshops and clubs. It was not an overnight job to become Whoopie Goldberg.

Discipline and rigorous attention to detail are necessary in almost any endeavor worth performing. It's not always easy to be constant. The temptation to allow the mundane to interfere can be tremendous, especially if you've spent a great deal of time folding laundry. It may be a lot easier to go clean out the fridge than to commit yourself to working on a painting, but if you are at core a painter, that is what you need to do.

Until recently, it was not always possible for a woman to fulfill herself through herself. Sometimes this was only possible through parent, husband, or child.

Not too long before age forced her to stop receiving the press, and not too far from the end of her life, I saw Rose Kennedy interviewed on television. Both the interviewer and Rose appeared aware that Rose was nearing the end of an extraordinary life, and many of the questions bore a "summing up" flavor. One of the questions and its answer sticks in my mind.

"Mrs. Kennedy," the interviewer began, "you have been associated with politics and politicians all your life. You have been the daughter of a politician, wife of a politician, and mother of politicians. You have been closely involved with these men as they participated in politics. You must have found great satisfaction in this."

" Yes, yes," said Mrs. Kennedy.

"But had things been otherwise, had other options been available to women then, would you have preferred to live your life as you did, or would you rather have done it yourself?"

Rose Kennedy only thought about it for a second. Then she looked directly into the camera and said, "Of course you are correct, things were as they were. But if it had been possible, if things had been otherwise, I'd rather have done it myself."

On a perfect June day my flight instructor and I were traversing the pattern around the Santa Fe airport. The "pattern" is the rectangle created by flying a rectangle around an airport, and its direction is determined by the runways in use, and that is determined by the direction of the wind.

I was riding high, as I had only the day before returned from the Biplane Fly-In at Bartlesville, over in eastern Oklahoma. I had been lucky enough while there to fly front cockpit in a World War I replica. There had been no instruments, just stick and rudder, and when I was allowed to take the controls, and flew over the lush green hills, wind in my face, it had been an dream come true. On the homeward trip back to the field we had engaged another biplane in a mock "dogfight," They later claimed to have shot us down, but we really knew we had shot them down.

Today the delicious June weather had held, and our climb out from the field had been a bit slow. Paul, my instructor, turned to me. "I know what would make it easier for you to fly today," he told me. "If I got out."

I turned to him aghast. "But, I mean, do you really think I'm ready?" I gulped.

He thought I was ready.

A little later I was taxiing by myself to runway three-three, and then out into takeoff position. I felt calm as I rose into the sky alone and started around the pattern. At one point someone cut me off while I was on the radio to the tower, but I kept my cool, and repeated myself. Three times I took off and landed as required, dealing with the other air traffic, speaking with the tower as needed. When finally I had landed and taxied off the runway, the tower congratulated the "occupant of zero-one-xray, who has just completed her first solo flight." I will never forget sitting alone in that cockpit in my yellow overall, taxiing back to tie-down position. I felt every age I had ever been all together. I felt a completeness I had never known.

"This is who I really am," I thought.

Later, back at the aviation building, then called Zia Aviation, people came running to see who had soloed. "Now you belong to the one percent of people in this country who have soloed," one young man told me. It was some time afterward that the thought occurred to me to wonder how many people of that one percent were grandmothers.

In the early days of flight, before radio, the instructor in the rear cockpit communicated with the student in the front cockpit by pulling on the tails of his shirt; right, left, up, down. So it was that, when a student soloed, the instructor, to indicate the student's new status, would cut off his shirt tails. Today, the tradition continues.

Paul ran to get scissors, and a few minutes later I was minus a large portion of the back of my shirt, and possessed of a piece of cotton bearing my name, the date, a picture of a happily landing plane, and Paul's name. The shirt was one I'd had for some time, and the front bore a phrase that had helped me get to this day. It said simply, "Women Fly."

Arlene in the Tiger Moth. Photo courtesy of Susan Larson.

CHAPTER NINE

With a special passion in your life, people often send along to you newspaper clippings that deal with a special interest.

So it happened that my son-in-law's parents who live in Tulsa, sent me an article from the local newspaper about a Tulsa resident who had built a totally authentic SE5 Nuport replica biplane which he has actually flown in the film about Howard Hughes, *The Aviator*.

Reading the article, I formulate lots of questions that I would like to ask Jack Kearbey, and eventually I phone him. Jack proves to be a genuinely helpful resource, always ready to pass on his expertise.

Because Jack has been married for more than fifty years to a gal who originally hailed from England, they frequently visit there, and when I tell him that I'll soon be taking a long-saved-for trip to the British Isles with a friend, it is Jack who tells me about the antique aircraft museum at Biggleswade. He tells me it is seventeen miles from the town of Duxford, where the American Air Museum, already on our schedule, is located.

The American Air Museum in Britain displays fighters and bombers, the "War Birds," from World War II. It is, an extraordinary coincidence that it is from this field at Duxford, where The American Air Museum in Britain has been built, that my cousin Howard flew his P47s.

The museum is a delight for a couple of pilots, and after we have toured it, I go alone to stand quietly beside the runway. In my mind's eye I see those shot-up P47s sputtering in to land in the British damp. I hear the engine of one skip a beat, and time for me slides backwards.

It's warm and sunny when we drive over to Biggleswade. This museum proves a joy to an enthusiast of early aircraft. These planes sometime fly on weekends, but it's Wednesday. However, I'm drawn to peer out at the grass airstrip in front of the museum, where an antique Tiger Moth is giving rides to some boys who are the equivalent of Boy Scouts.

Suddenly I notice my friend Susan out there with the plane that has just landed. She is talking to the pilots, and I waste no time running out to join them.

"Where have you been?" Susan calls out as I run up. "I've just arranged with these guys to take you up!" I can scarcely believe it as I slip on the goggles and helmet with microphone and earphones, and climb into the front cockpit. We roll out over the green English grass, and lift above the fields of England.

For me there is no flying like open-cockpit flying and as we glide over the countryside, I am in heaven, and can't imagine anything better. Then the pilot says something over the radio, but it's garbled, and I can't understand. "Please say again," I tell him.

"I said," the pilot tells me, "it's your airplane."

I can't believe it, but grab the stick, feet on the rudder pedals, and watching the yellowed instruments, let her have her way. She turns a complete left circle before I take command. She requires a firm hand, but responds, and, in heaven before, I have now entered some unknown and completely over-the-top dimension.

Something I've mentioned before is the Biplane Fly-In, held at Bartlesville, over in eastern Oklahoma in early June. It's my favorite fly-in.

Anyone who arrives in a plane that is not a biplane must park way down beyond the third hangar, and the biplanes, parked on the June grass of the flight line, give a feeling of going back in time. It seems as if I've become a part of those early years of flying that are sometimes referred to as "the golden era of flight."

There is a large tent where tables and chairs have been set up, and where people go to eat the "funnel cakes" and "greasy hamburgers" advertised by the food booths, while they watch the biplanes take off and land from the grass between the runways. Many of the pilots are eager to give rides, or to fly in formation with other pilots of the same type of aircraft.

On Friday night there is a supper in this tent, with the guest of honor for the year and other local dignitaries, and on Saturday night the awards dinner is held in an elegant downtown hotel. During the day various workshops dealing with different aspects of building or flying biplanes are held.

It is here in Bartlesville that I finally meet Jack Kearbey. His plane appears to have flown in directly from some World War I dogfight, and as I examine it, I am astounded by the superb workmanship.

Other experienced "experimental" builders, ("experimental" is the term designated by the Federal Aircraft Administration for home-built), gravitate to Jack's plane, and listening to them is for me a learning experience.

One time it rains, and some of these pilots sit with Jack and me under the wing of his plane waiting for the rain to stop, when, it seems, Jack will take off into another time and place.

It is after I have moved the plane and established my new and astonishing workshop there in the EAA hangar in Los Alamos, that I receive a call from Jack. He tells me he has just mailed me a list of parts that he wishes me to order and have sent to him from Wick's Aircraft Supply. I have been picking Jack's brain for some time regarding who might possibly construct my landing gear. Now, to my sheer delight, Jack informs me he has decided to build it himself.

Again and once again the "invisible hands reach out to help."

My workshop in the hangar in Los Alamos is a joy. I love the vast extent of my power tools (and this is the person who built sixty-eight wing ribs with no power tools, with just the determination to have her own airplane), and I love running to watch every time a plane lands or takes off. Occasionally someone comes in to announce that they are "going up" for a few minutes, and would I like to come?

One day as I am cleaning up the workbench, one of the small, curled scraps from my beautiful drill press catches in my finger. These scraps are all over the place, and they are a menace. It's all too clear that I need a good shop vacuum. I set off up the street to Metzgar's Hardware store, where I stand eyeing the shop vacs. The large, multi-purpose one I favor is much too expensive, and I stand, contemplating all the possibilities, unsure what to do.

"Psst, psst."

I turn to see a strange man standing behind me, signaling. He speaks out of the corner of his mouth, whispering, glancing furtively around.

"Would you consider buying a used shop vac?"

"You have one for sale?"

"I got five for sale."

"How come you have five for sale?"

"I fix stuff. I just live a couple a blocks from here. If you're interested, follow me."

I do, and twenty minutes later I own the large, multi-purpose shop vac that I had coveted. As of this writing, it is still working well.

I am lying on my back looking up through the frame of the right bottom wing to the tin roof. A red and blue umbrella stands guard over the TV and some of the tools on the workbench, but the TV, which had been running again the story of Wilbur and Orville at Kitty Hawk, has been turned off, since the torrent pounding on the tin roof of the hangar makes hearing anything else impossible.

I am taking a break. The drops that leak through the hangar roof don't bother me. I will need to get up onto the roof again come fall and seal over all the nail holes, but so what. I am not really lying on my back on an old mat on the hangar floor, I am actually lying on cloud nine. Out of the corner of my eye I can see Dreamcatcher's landing gear, delivered yesterday by Jack Kearbey's friends Sam and Dorothy Tally, who were traveling through town on their way to Montana. The breathtaking workmanship Jack has put into this has me spellbound as it sits proudly on its motorcycle tires, its intricately woven wire wheels twinkling. For all the painstakingly careful work Jack has put into this he will accept no money at all, only reimbursement for the parts.

This beautiful piece of machinery has so captivated me that when it arrived I felt like a child who wants to take her new toy to bed, and had felt a particularly strong urge to put my sleeping bag down beside it and spend the night in the hangar.

From the very start of this project I had tried to make myself face the fact that due to the very magnitude of what I was attempting, there would be times when things would go very wrong. Now the first real setback has presented itself.

The owner of the place from which I had first purchased steel had thought that stainless steel was nearly as strong as 4130 chromoly, which the plans required. Because it was so clean to handle and did not need scrubbing and coating with zinc chromate, I had chosen it. Now the EAA tech consultants, and indeed all the guys whose opinion I trusted, have told me this as not true. Stainless is only about a third as strong, and to boot, the holes, drilled in long hours of tedious metal work, have not been done correctly. They need to be drilled a size smaller than required, then drilled the correct size with a bit called a "reamer," to ensure accuracy. Most of the metalwork must be removed, rebent, reground, refurnished, drilled properly, and replaced. It proves to be an orgy of removal, tagging, marking, reworking and installing. My only consolation is that this has been discovered now, before assembly.

Just when I need both hands for this work, Santa Fe is deluged with three

The typed manuscript ends here.

The adobe house where Arlene lived and started to build her plane. The photo was taken four days after Arlene's death.

Post Script

In her handwritten notes for the *Sky's the Limit*, Arlene outlines that the cold and unusual amounts of snow during the winter of 2006/2007 had slowed the project down. Further, her last notes lament the fact that just as she really needed both hands for the metal work that had to be done to the connection plates on her airplane, she slipped on the ice and broke her left hand. The break in her hand also put a stop to the manuscript because she could not type. One week before her death, she was talking about how much she was looking forward to getting back to work on the manuscript now that her hand was almost completely healed.

On the last day of May, 2007, Arlene was driving by herself to one of her favorite events, the Bartlesville Fly-In, held each year in Bartlesville, Oklahoma. She left home before dawn and stopped at a diner for breakfast. Sometime mid-morning, near Clayton, New Mexico, she fell unconscious behind the wheel and her car crossed the meridian, crashed through a guardrail and she was killed instantly. A motorcyclist who was traveling in the opposite direction witnessed the accident and stopped to see if there was anything he could do to help. When it was clear to him that the accident had been fatal, he waited for the police in order to describe exactly what he saw. We, Arlene's family, are extremely grateful to this stranger who stopped to help and who was able to give us the details of what happened.

The autopsy pointed to either a cardiac event or minor stroke as the cause for Arlene's falling unconscious.

Arlene's plane at the time of her death.

Aftermath

Immediately after Arlene's death, my father and I flew out and met my brother, Artie, in Albuquerque where Arlene's body had been moved after the accident. My sister with a brand new baby, stayed in close touch by phone. As we began the process of sorting her possessions and dealing with the end of life "stuff" that needs to be done, we were helped tremendously by many of the wonderful friends with whom my mother surrounded herself.

Ginny Kahn generously loaned us the use of her nearby house to use as a base from which to organize ourselves. Karl Bottjer was a terrific help; Trudy Lawler, Arlene's landlady could not have been sweeter or more helpful, even bringing by food for us. Susan Larson provided constant support, finding temporary shelter for Mom's cats, checking in regularly, and offering assistance at every turn.

In addition, we received help from Arlene's neighbors and my stepmother Daphne Walsh, who helped enormously by phone, organizing movers, and even making restaurant reservations for meals we might have otherwise skipped. My sister, Amory, was torn by wanting to be in Santa Fe with us, and not wanting to expose her two-month-old baby to extensive travel or to leave him. As it turned out her physical separation from us allowed her to provide, by phone, a more objective perspective about what needed to be done.

One recurring concern we all had was what would happen to Arlene's plane? The EAA chapter at Los Alamos very generously allowed the plane to stay where it was in the EAA hangar at the Los Alamos airport until we could come up with a plan for it. Further, a well-attended memorial/remembrance service was held several months after her death at the hangar, which would have pleased Arlene no end.

As things evolved and the three of us, her children, talked, it became clear that what we all wanted was to find some way for someone to finish building Mom's plane. The simplest thing to do seemed to be to donate the half-built plane to her EAA chapter. They seemed convinced that they could find someone to take over the project. In the end, the concept was about the only simple part of this process.

It turns out that giving away the pieces of a partially-built aircraft is not something that the legal profession is regularly asked to do. Finding legal precedents, drafting language, and even getting the legal names and non-profit status of all the parties involved took time. Additionally, my brother Arthur who was dealing with most of this stuff was also renovating and moving into a new home, while trying to sort through and store all of Mom's furniture, most of her books, papers and photographs, as well as taking care of her two cats and two pet snakes.

Finally the papers were handed over and the process of finding a home for the plane could start in earnest. Jeff Scott and Roger Smith from the EAA Chapter that Mom belonged to, had been wonderfully patient and encouraging, but I think we all felt that finding someone to take on Mom's plane and complete it as she had intended seemed unlikely. Mom's plane is an "Aerial," a fairly rare biplane-adaptation of the slightly more common 1928 Pietenpol Sky Camper. It seemed more likely that different builders of Sky Campers would want different parts of Mom's Aerial. It was not what Arlene had wanted, but at least the EAA chapter would get their hangar space back and the parts would get used.

It therefore came as a huge surprise to hear from Jeff Scott that the plane was being shipped to Anchorage, Alaska, where students at the Begich Middle School would complete it as an Aerial. We could not believe it. When I told my sister over the phone we were both nearly in tears, this was so fitting and so perfect. Arlene's love of teaching children, her enthusiasm for flying, and her love of the Aerial were all coming together into one package. As we talked about the events that had led to this fitting tribute to Mom's wishes we ended up by laughing together; Arlene's belief that everything works out the way it is supposed to was so strong that although we know she would have been thrilled by the turn of events, we don't think she would have been the least surprised.

As the details emerged, it became clear that Arlene's plane had found a home through the generosity of a number of aviation enthusiasts from all over the country. Like most things that just "fall together," it appeared that the journey that took Arlene's plane from northern New Mexico to Anchorage, Alaska, was also the result of a lot of different people putting in a lot of hard work. This long chain of events was best summed up in an article by Clancey Maloney that appeared in the 2009 May/June issue of *99 News*, the official magazine of the International Organization of Women Pilots. The article is entitled *"Arlene Walsh Lives On Through the Legacy of Dreamcatcher, Her Big-Wing Taildragger."* The article is reprinted here with the permission of the author, Clancey Maloney, and the permission of *99 News*.

Arlene Walsh Lives On Through the Legacy of Dreamcatcher, Her Big-Wing Taildragger

BY CLANCEY MALONEY, *Rio Grande Norte Chapter*

"Wow, look at all the pieces of wood! This must have taken a lot of time," exclaimed Dylan Rubery, 14, an eighth grader at Begich Middle School in Anchorage, Alaska.

Dylan was present as the Pietenpol Aerial, a big-wing taildragger named Dreamcatcher, was unveiled on the Begich gymnasium stage. The aircraft had belonged to Arlene Walsh of the Rio Grande Norte Chapter who was killed in a single-car accident on May 30, 2007, en route to the National Biplane Expo in Bartlesville, Oklahoma. Dylan and his classmates plan to finish the project Walsh began years before as an educational tool for her own pupils and for herself.

Arlene Walsh's life was all about kids, airplanes and flying. Walsh, 71, was a Rio Grande Norte Future Woman Pilot and kindergarten teacher. Her legacies are not just the knowledge and enthusiasm she delivered to her pupils but also her love of aviation and the airplane she was building when she died.

According to her obituary in **The Santa Fe New Mexican**, Walsh fell in love with aviation listening to her three older cousins' stories of their World War II flying exploits. She raised her children and managed a long teaching career in Massachusetts before moving to Santa Fe, New Mexico, in 1985. She taught at The Little School in nearby Cerrillos, New Mexico, soon becoming head teacher. Transferring to St. Francis of Assisi Cathedral School in Santa Fe, she taught there until the school closed in 2006. Walsh's final year teaching was part-time at the Garcia Street Club Preschool.

One pupil's parent, writing in a **Santa Fe New Mexican** commentary piece, said, "In her kindergarten class, kids learned the names of stars...the life cycle of water. Overriding all was Miss Arlene's love of flying. [Her class] went to the Santa Fe Airport every year. And they saw a grandmother—still working to make her dream possible, building her own airplane, studying for her pilot's license."

A perpetual student pilot with 200 or so hours, Walsh kept a poster of a Cessna 152 cockpit on the classroom wall, at kids' height, along with an old headset, so that her pint-sized pupils could pretend they were flying.

Pint-sized herself, Walsh started building her Pietenpol Aerial, Dreamcatcher, after her move to Santa Fe. She especially wanted to use the airplane as an educational project to encourage her pupils' interest in aviation. A modified version of one of the first homebuilt aircraft, originally designed in 1928 by Bernie Pietenpol, the Aerial was a two-place parasol—an airplane whose fuselage is suspended under the upper wing by a set of struts and/or cables.

Progress on the Aerial came in fits and starts, along with moves from her living room and porch to various workshops and hangars. After years in a small commercial park, Arlene moved the skeletal fuselage, empennage and wings to an EAA hangar at Los Alamos Airport (KLAM). Only a short while later, Arlene was gone, and Dreamcatcher languished.

Settling her estate, her children Ted Walsh of Conway, New Hampshire, Arthur Walsh of Albuquerque, New Mexico, and Amory Walsh Hartman of River Edge, New Jersey, sold the pieces to Texan Oscar Zuniga. Because Zuniga needed only the landing gear and wheels to complete his own project aircraft, the rest of the Aerial was left in the EAA hangar at Los Alamos.

Back in September of 2008, Begich Middle School students watched and listened to Barrington Irving's story of his solo around-the-world flight in his Columbia 400. Irving, the first African-American pilot to fly solo around the world, was in Alaska to tell of his experiences during his 2007 flight. Part of his presentation showed Alaska's Hooper Bay High School and their "Build A Plane" project. Inspired and excited, the Begich students wanted to build their own.

Middle-school principal Jeanne Fischer searched for a project airplane, seeking advice from Angie Slingluff, the Federal Aviation

Administration (FAA) Aviation and Space Education coordinator in Anchorage.

Intrigued, Angie contacted Rod Stapleton, a member of both Alaska Airmen's Association and EAA's Anchorage Chapter. Stapleton put out an Internet request for a project aircraft, and Dreamcatcher's new owner, Oscar Zuniga, answered the call.

"Be careful what you ask for because you may find yourself paying to ship a project to Alaska from some faraway place," Oscar told Rod Stapleton.

When Angie learned about Dreamcatcher, something sounded familiar. In July, 2008, she had met Susan Larson, then Ninety-Nines International Vice President, at the annual Conference in Anchorage. Susan had told Angie about Arlene's recent death and her airplane. Upon hearing about the Dreamcatcher, Angie put two and two together and called Susan, who confirmed that the airplane was indeed Arlene's.

Susan and Arlene met in 2002 after Susan's move to Santa Fe from California. Arlene's small adobe apartment was barely a block from Susan's vintage adobe in Santa Fe. Although they met during the annual spring cleaning of the local irrigation ditch, a Lenten tradition in New Mexico, the story they liked to tell was that Susan saw Arlene working on the wooden wing ribs on her porch, heating the ribs over a steaming pot in her kitchen so they would bend to conform to the jigs.

"The wing ribs were hung from the living room log beams," said Susan. "Walsh's building an airplane was all the more amazing because she had yet to pass her private pilot check ride." The two soon became good friends and charter members of the Rio Grande Norte Chapter. Meanwhile, in December of 2008, Rod Stapleton contacted Harry McDonald, a pilot, aircraft owner and also the owner of Carlile Transportation Services (CTS). Harry owned a trucking terminal in Texas that made regular runs to Canada via Albuquerque. He immediately agreed that CTS would carry Dreamcatcher to Anchorage for free if Rod could arrange for crating.

Angie put Rod in touch with Susan, who volunteered to oversee the crating. Jeff Scott of the Los Alamos FAA chapter volunteered the chapter's labor to crate the airplane. The Anchorage EAA chapter supplied the funding for crating materials, and CTS picked Dreamcatcher up at KLAM in January, 2009. She was on her way to Alaska!

In early March, 2009, to much drama, fanfare and spotlights on the school stage, Dreamcatcher made her debut at Begich Middle School.

Principal Jeanne Fischer explained, "Look at all the cutting, carving and gluing, but this aircraft is only a little under half completed. It will be up to you, the students, to finish it." They will work on the aircraft with volunteer aircraft builders on Saturdays and over the summer.

In Anchorage, pilot and Begich Middle School teacher Dan Carey, who will instruct the students on aircraft construction, met and formed the Begich Build A Plane Steering Committee to organize and oversee the Dreamcatcher project. In January, the committee members, including the principal, other teachers, Angie, Alaska Airmen's Association executive director Dee Hanson, Rod, and Dominic Balappa, an airline pilot, certificated flight instructor and airframe-and-powerplant technician, met to plan the work on Dreamcatcher.

The mahogany and spruce Dreamcatcher lacked an engine, propeller, cowling, landing gear and wheels, rigging, struts and instruments. She'll also need seats, fabric covering, fuel system and tanks, an electrical system and a paint job. Anchorage EAA chapter member Lars Gleitsmann queried Kevin Alexander, assistant professor of aviation maintenance at the University of Alaska/Fairbanks, about an engine for donation to the project.

Alexander had an engine—a rebuilt 0-290—that would become Dreamcatcher's heart. One major component down, numerous to go.

"I have 10 pages in this notebook of people and local businesses that have supported getting this project started!" said Principal Fischer.

"This is an amazing story," said the principal. "The wooden control sticks have a Native American dreamcatcher etched into their tops."

The Rio Grande Norte Ninety-Nines already know Dreamcatcher's true heart will always belong to Arlene Walsh and not to the metal engine. Susan said it best in an e-mail to Angie last December, "Arlene would love to know Dreamcatcher is being finished by students." The Rio Grande Norte Ninety-Nines are certain Arlene is watching over.

Unattributed quotes originally appeared in **The Transponder**, a publication of the Alaska Airmen's Association.

Acknowledgements

When I first came up with the idea of melding these three manuscripts into a memoir, I had no idea that it was going to take more than two years to complete this endeavor. I doubt that I would have ever persevered had it not been for the encouragement of my family and Arlene's many friends. In particular, I would like to thank Susan Larson and Ginny Kahn for their support and through all aspects of this project.

I would also like to thank Jean and George Hurley for their close reading of the galley and their many helpful observations and suggestions. Their help was the final push I needed to see this book to completion.

Ted Walsh
Conway, NH